THE ATLAS OF HUMAN HISTORY

THE FIRST SETTLERS

Where Stone Age peoples settled, built homes and grew crops

Devised and produced by
Andrea Dué
Text by
Renzo Rossi

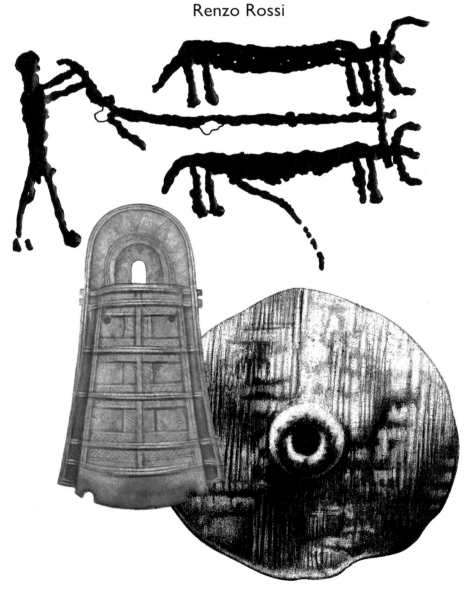

CHERRYTREE BOOKS

INTRODUCTION

A Cherrytree Book

First published by Jaca Book
© Editoríale Jaca Book Spa, Milano
1993

This edition published 1995
by Cherrytree Press Ltd
Windsor Bridge Road
Bath, Avon BA2 3AX

Copyright © Cherrytree Press Ltd 1995

Text by Renzo Rossi
Translation by Patricia Borlenghi
Edited by Brian Williams
Maps by Alessandro Bartolozzi,
Roberto Simoni, Rosanna Rea
Colour illustrations by Andrea Dué,
Roberto Simoni, Giorgio Bacchin,
Giuseppe Cicio
Black and white illustrations by Andrea
Dué, Elisabetta Giulianni, Chiara
Pignaris, Rosanna Rea
Produced by AS Publishing

British Library Cataloguing in
Publication Data
Rossi, Renzo
  The First Settlers. – (Atlas of Human
History Series)
  I. Title II. Dué, Andrea III. Series
  930

ISBN 0-7451-5255-4

Printed and bound in Italy by Grafiche
Editoríali Padane Spa, Cremona

The first true human beings lived in caves. They ate what they could find or kill, and protected themselves from harsh weather and wild beasts as best they could. Slowly these people developed skills and made discoveries that enabled them to leave their caves, build homes and make clothes for themselves, and begin to shape their environment. This development happened in the Middle East around 10,000 BC, after the last Ice Age when the world's climate became less harsh. With milder weather, plants multiplied. There was plenty for people to eat, so populations grew. People moved to new places. Many gave up the wandering life of hunter-gatherers and settled in one place, building villages. To supplement the food they got from hunting and fishing, people gathered wild grain and stored it to eat during the winter months. Eventually they began to plant the grain and so, around 8000 BC, farming began.

At the same time people began to think about themselves and the world around them, and express their thoughts in pictures. They created statues of pregnant females, Mother Goddesses that symbolized fertility, and pictures of bulls that symbolized the male's role in creation. The tools these people used were made of stone and the period of their history is known as the New Stone Age, or Neolithic Period. Expert toolmakers, they discovered how to fire clay pots in ovens to harden them. They lived in organized communities, growing crops, rearing domestic animals, and trading with one another. As people started to trade goods, they invented writing and number systems to enable them to keep records of their deals. Villages grew into towns, some with as many as 5,000 people.

By 5,000 years ago there were flourishing civilizations in Mesopotamia, Egypt, the Indus Valley and China. Around 3300 BC the Bronze Age began in Mesopotamia. The discovery of metals accelerated the pace of change and brought power and wealth to those who could mine and work them. Copper and bronze tools replaced stone ones, and metals were also used to make weapons and armour for soldiers. Across much of Asia, Africa and Europe (the regions on which this book mostly concentrates), populations were on the move, seeking new lands, taking with them their beliefs and languages. Cultures mingled. Religion became a powerful force in human affairs and its importance is reflected in buildings, in social systems and in art.

The first civilizations of the ancient world left a rich legacy, now being revealed by modern archaeologists and scholars. This volume of THE ATLAS OF HUMAN HISTORY makes use of such evidence in its maps, full-colour reconstructions and other illustrations.

B.W.

CONTENTS

1 THE WORLD AT THE END OF THE LAST ICE AGE

Europe at the start of the Holocene Epoch, about 10,000 years ago

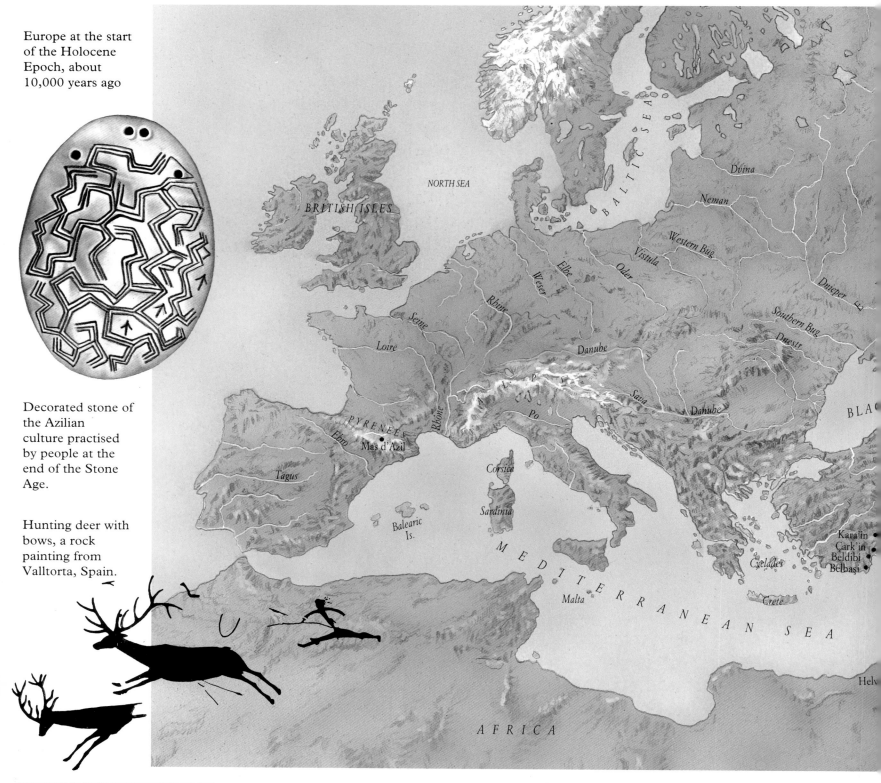

Decorated stone of the Azilian culture practised by people at the end of the Stone Age.

Hunting deer with bows, a rock painting from Valltorta, Spain.

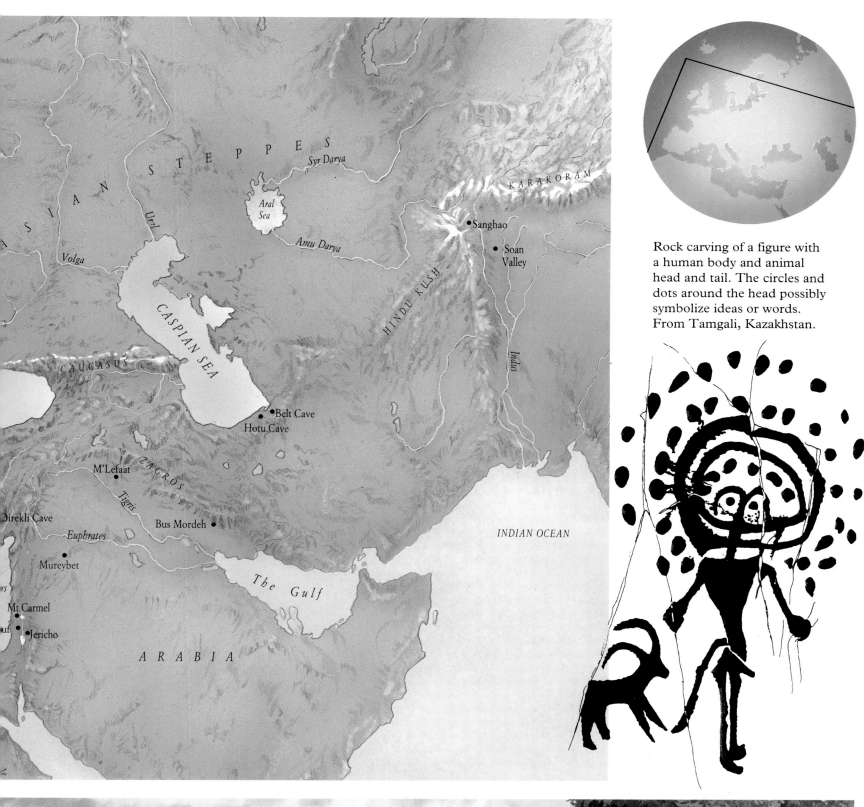

Rock carving of a figure with a human body and animal head and tail. The circles and dots around the head possibly symbolize ideas or words. From Tamgali, Kazakhstan.

1 THE WORLD AT THE END OF THE LAST ICE AGE

A basketwork trap, still used in parts of the world to catch fish. Fish swim in through the funnel-mouth in the base.

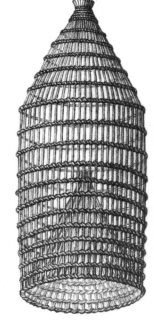

Around 10,000 years ago, the earth's climate became milder and the post-glacial period began. This marked the start of the Holocene Epoch – the latest division of the Quaternary Period (one of the periods of geological time, measured in millions of years) and the epoch in which we are living now. The rise in temperature at the end of the Ice Age resulted in a change in the natural environment.

A new landscape

The melting glaciers retreated across Eurasia and America to the extreme north or to high mountains. Rivers swelled with melted ice and ocean levels began to rise, flooding low-lying coasts. With more seawater evaporating in the higher temperatures, there was a huge increase in rainfall and vegetation grew far more vigorously. Birch trees and conifers first took over the vast areas left bare by the retreating glaciers, and were then replaced by oak, beech, willow and walnut trees.

This open forest encouraged the spread of animals such as red deer, elk, wild boar and aurochs (wild cattle), but was no longer suitable for the migratory herds of reindeer which moved northwards to follow the mosses and lichens of the retreating tundra.

New challenges for humankind

Life for humans should have been easier. But in fact traditional food resources became scarcer. Animals used to a cold environment moved north (like the reindeer) or (like the mammoth) died out. People had to make do

Fragment of a wooden oar, from the lakeside settlement of Star Carr (Yorkshire) in Britain, and a flint axe used for making canoes.

with more modest food supplies. They hunted smaller animals, especially deer or wild boar, and ate shellfish and land snails – as we know from the enormous deposits of shells they left in waste heaps, or middens.

There was a decline in cultural activities, such as art, which had developed during the earlier part of the Stone Age, and in toolmaking. Traditional methods of making stone and bone tools developed no further, for example.

A village on the lower Danube River (pictured in colour on pages 4/5), after the glaciers retreated. The villagers' huts, supported on poles and covered in animal skins, stand on the riverbank in the middle of conifer and birch forest.

Two hunters set to work skinning a deer with flint knives.

The meat will be smoked to preserve it. Women use bone needles to sew animal skins. Deer antlers and bones are valued for toolmaking. An elder of the village, perhaps no longer able to hunt, saws bone to make harpoons for fishing, tools and ornaments. A hunter with a stone-tipped spear watches

admiringly, perhaps hoping for a new ornament to add to the chain of animal teeth he wears around his neck.

Three other men are busy making a boat from a tree-trunk, hollowed out with axes and with fire. On the riverbank, men and women fish with their hands or with harpoons, but also with

basketwork traps. Two boys dig in the earth with sticks looking for snails and other edible creatures. The return of hunters who have shot a wild boar with their bows means plenty of meat for all.

TOOLS AND INVENTIONS OF THIS PERIOD

1 axe   7 knotted net
2 scalpel } made from   8 pottery vase from
3 pick   } deer antler   Ertebolle, Denmark
4 hoe   9 birch bow
5 float   10 spear with crosswise
6 weight for fishing net   point

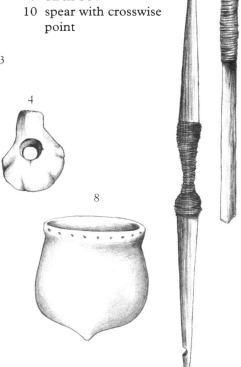

The bow made hunters more successful in killing herds of wild animals.
Above: Hunters shooting deer, from a rock painting in Spain.
Below: Men with bows and arrows, also from a cave in Spain.

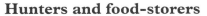

Hunters and food-storers

Human hunters used bows and arrows, as well as spears, clubs and stones. With large prey such as mammoths no longer available, hunters often killed smaller animals indiscriminately, slaughtering whole herds when they could trap them. Cave paintings show hunting of this kind, dispelling the idea that Stone Age hunters 'farmed' wild animals by selective killing. Hunters probably tamed wild dogs to help them.

The dogs no doubt shared the people's meals of snails, mussels and clams, which formed an important part of the human diet, especially in North Africa. Waste dumps of as many as 80 million shells found in Algeria suggest that shellfish were a useful food source. But even more important were plants. People ate seeds, fruit, vegetables (peas, lentils, chickpeas, leeks, asparagus), thistles and wild grasses (millet, barley, wild wheat).

Humans learned to store such foods, and food-storing – which began about 10,000 years ago – was a feature of the Natuf culture of Palestine and southern Syria. This marked the start of a new form of life – settlement in one place.

This painting from Castillo in Spain shows a woman collecting honey from a wild bees' nest. It is painted in red ochre.

A collection of human skulls, found in a cave burial in northern Europe. The different skull types suggest that several distinct types of humans were living together.

2 CHANGES IN THE LATER STONE AGE

The map shows the spread of agriculture across Europe and the Middle East.

- Up to 10,000 years ago
- Up to 9,000 years ago
- Up to 8,000 years ago
- Up to 7,000 years ago

A Stone Age picture of a man holding a tool of unknown purpose. He wears a short tunic and a pointed hat. From Ramat Matred in Palestine.

The cultivation of wild cereals spread in a crescent from the Mediterranean to The Gulf.

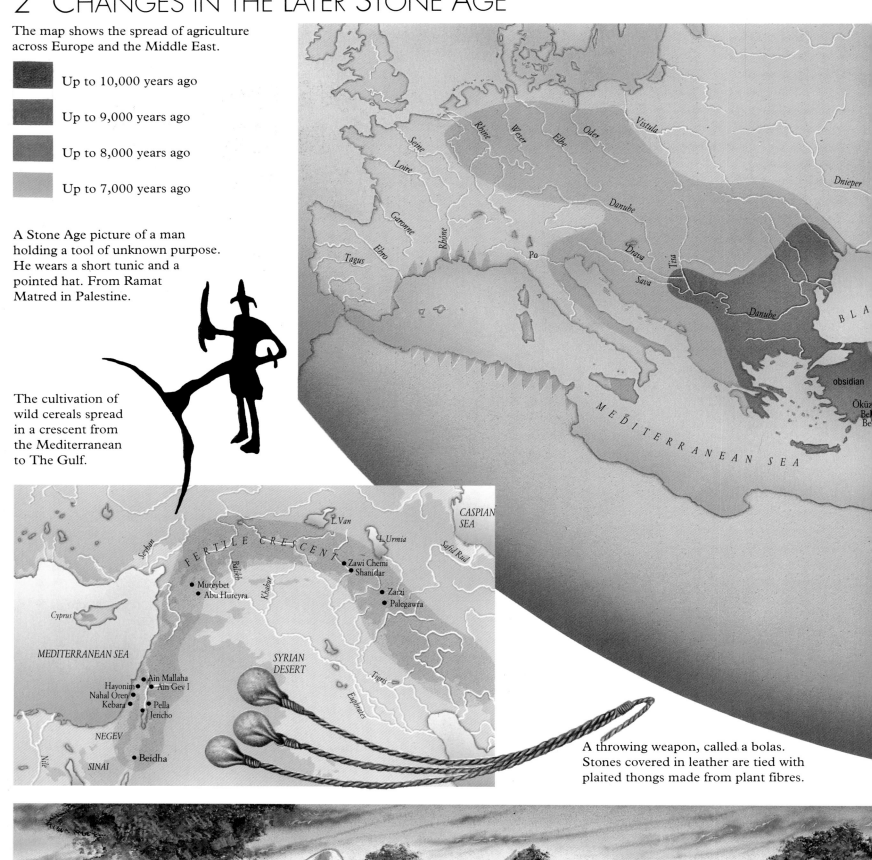

A throwing weapon, called a bolas. Stones covered in leather are tied with plaited thongs made from plant fibres.

A picture of a wild goat (top), a human (above left) and another animal (above right) from a cave in Palandi, Anatolia, Turkey.

A wild ox and a human, probably in a hunting scene, from Anatolia.

9

2 Changes in the Later Stone Age

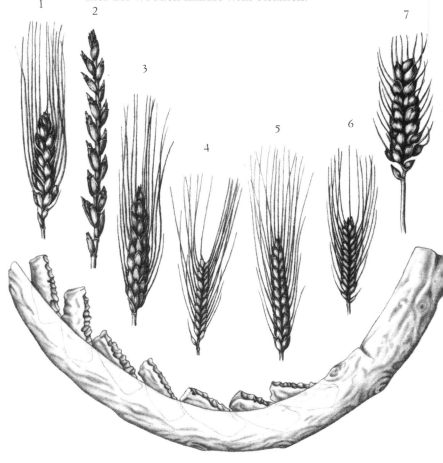

Around the shores of the Mediterranean, first in the east and then in the west, there was a great change in human life between 10,000 and 8,000 years ago. The change was great enough to be compared with that of the Industrial Revolution of recent times. In less than two thousand years, human existence changed more profoundly than in the preceding two million years.

Human beings began a new relationship with their environment. People stopped the destructive and indiscriminate use of natural resources, through large-scale hunting, and began to adapt to the reproductive cycles of plants and animals, using them as we do today, to produce food. Agriculture began, and the domestication of animals, leading to crop and stock farming and to a 'mixed economy' of farming and simple industry – making goods for trade. This change affected the way people lived together, and the way in which they thought about religion and culture.

The first farmers

Until quite recently, most experts thought that the beginning of agriculture was the major cause of permanent settlement, because farmers had to live near the lands they cultivated. Today, further studies have suggested that people built permanent villages to live in before they took to growing crops and rearing animals.

Around 12,000 years ago the Natufians of Syria and Palestine were already living in organized groups in permanent huts, yet they were still at the stage before agriculture had developed. It was not the cultivation of the land that led humans to stay in one place. The opposite happened. It was staying in one place that forced people to select and grow the seeds of edible plants, and to domesticate and then breed certain animals.

Agriculture proper started slowly in the 'Fertile Crescent' – the semicircle of land in the Middle East from Palestine in the west to what are now Iraq and Iran in the east. People who until then had lived as hunter-

This reconstruction of a farming village (pictured in colour on pages 8/9) is based on finds at Mureybet in Syria. Men and women harvest ears of corn and barley with flint reaping-hooks set in wooden handles. They carry the grain in baskets to the village, where it is stored to feed the inhabitants until the next harvest. A hunter returns with a hare he has shot with his bow, accompanied by his invaluable companion, a dog.

In the village live other domestic animals. Sheep gather around a drinking trough, watched over by a sheepdog. Other sheep are grazing on the hillside, watched by a shepherd.

A new house is being built. It is round and about 6 metres (19ft) across, divided inside by low partitions into separate areas for cooking, sleeping, food storage and animals. The wooden framework of the house is covered in a mixture of clay, stones and straw. For walls, a new building material is being used – mud brick, made by hand and dried in the sun.

Other villagers are shaping crude clay pots and bowls, for storing liquids and grain. When finished, the pots will be fired in an oven, making them much harder and longer-lasting.

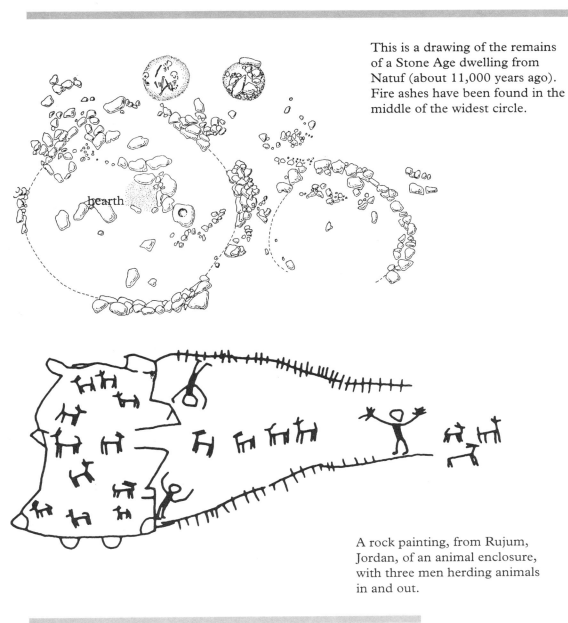

This is a drawing of the remains of a Stone Age dwelling from Natuf (about 11,000 years ago). Fire ashes have been found in the middle of the widest circle.

hearth

THE TAMING OF THE DOG
The wild ancestor of the domestic dog, like the jackal of today, was a frequent visitor to human camps and settlements. When dogs and humans gradually began to live side by side, and eat the same food, people realized the advantages that could be gained from the dog's dependence on them. Dog and human adapted to each other, as is shown in evidence from many parts of the world. Bones thought to be dog bones have been found with human remains dating back 12,000 years in the Dordogne (France) and in Palegawra (Iran). Just as old is a burial in Mallaha (Israel), where a young dog was placed in the arms of a dead boy. Dog bones of a similar age have also been discovered in Jaguar Cave, Idaho, USA.

A rock painting, from Rujum, Jordan, of an animal enclosure, with three men herding animals in and out.

1 The skull of an inhabitant of Jericho, in Jordan. The face is covered in painted clay and shells were placed in the eye sockets – presumably as part of the burial ceremony.
2 A plan of the ancient city of Jericho, perhaps the oldest continuously lived-in town (from 11,000 years ago). The Stone Age town covered an area of three hectares (7.4 acres) and was home to about 16,000 people. It was defended by a stone wall and a ditch.
3 The circular tower built in the walls of Jericho, cut away to show the steep stairs inside.

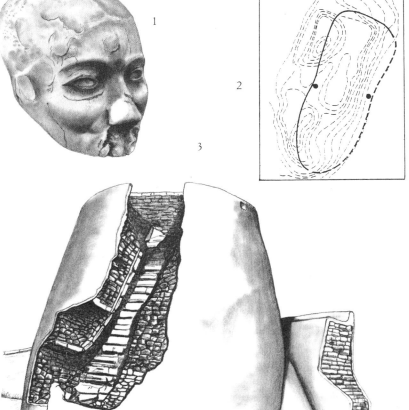

gatherers started to grow wheat and barley, which grew wild. To these crops, they soon added peas, lentils, beans and vetch.

Domestic animals

About the same time, animal-rearing began in the same region, with people keeping goats and sheep. Afterwards came the breeding of pigs and then donkeys and cattle. The tame hunting dog was later trained to become a sheepdog, and the horse was domesticated, probably for the first time in what is now southern Russia.

From 7,000 years ago, farming communities existed in the Middle East. Villages and small towns of dwellings with mud walls or made from mud bricks were organized in permanent settlements. They were based on a fairly advanced farming system, which did not solely depend on the richness of the local soil.

Agriculture arrived in Europe from the Fertile Crescent, spreading along the coastal routes of the Mediterranean Sea and northwards along the River Danube. It was spread by a movement of people and also as a result of cultural changes which occurred at about the same time (8,000-9,000 years ago) in Southwest Asia and Central America – where people were also becoming farmers.

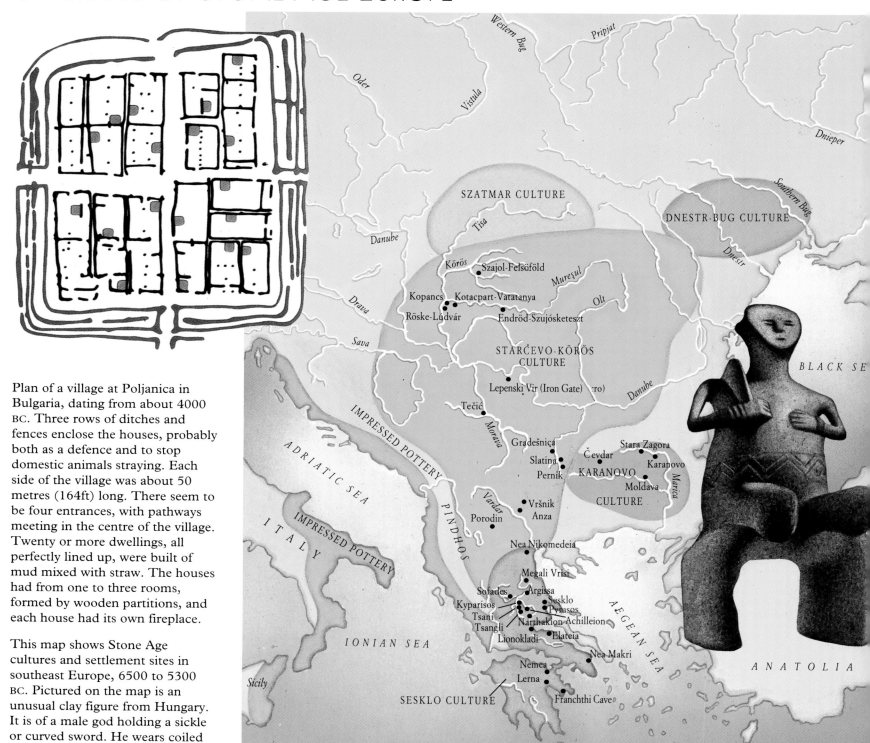

Plan of a village at Poljanica in Bulgaria, dating from about 4000 BC. Three rows of ditches and fences enclose the houses, probably both as a defence and to stop domestic animals straying. Each side of the village was about 50 metres (164ft) long. There seem to be four entrances, with pathways meeting in the centre of the village. Twenty or more dwellings, all perfectly lined up, were built of mud mixed with straw. The houses had from one to three rooms, formed by wooden partitions, and each house had its own fireplace.

This map shows Stone Age cultures and settlement sites in southeast Europe, 6500 to 5300 BC. Pictured on the map is an unusual clay figure from Hungary. It is of a male god holding a sickle or curved sword. He wears coiled bracelets and a belt is his only clothing. A mask hides his face.

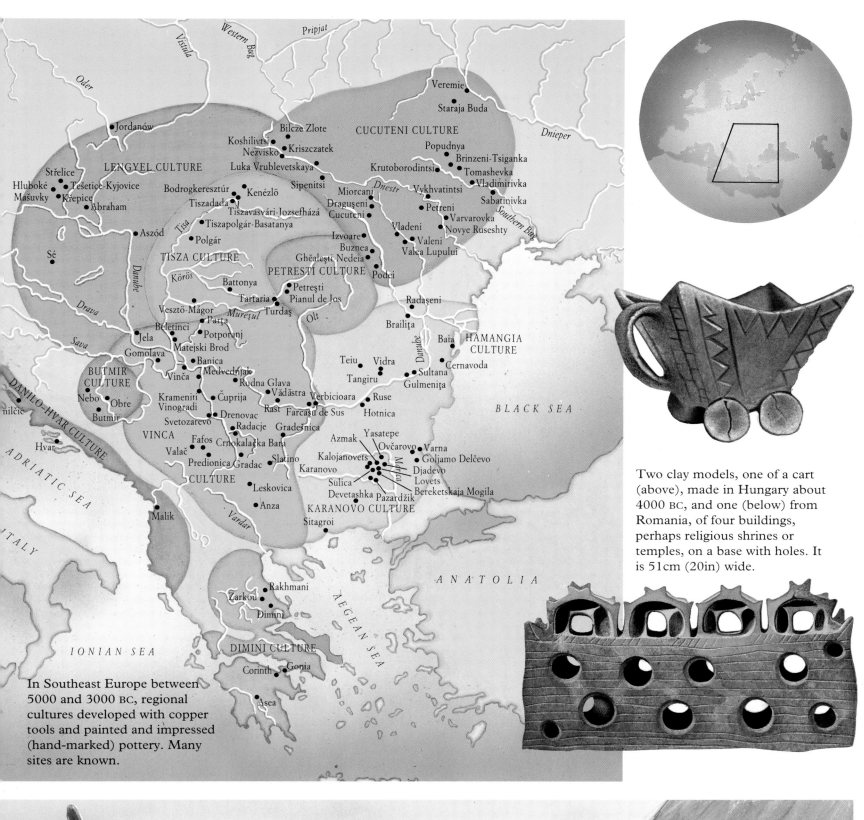

CUCUTENI CULTURE

LENGYEL CULTURE

Veremie
Staraja Buda
Popudnya
Brinzeni-Tsiganka
Bilcze Zlote
Koshilivtsi
Nezvisko
Kriszczatek
Luka Vrublevetskaya
Krutoborodintsi
Tomashevka
Vladimirivka
Jordanów
Strelice
Hluboké
Tešetice-Kyjovice
Mašuvky
Křepice
Abraham
Bodrogkeresztúr
Kenézlő
Tiszadada
Tiszavasvári-Jozsefházá
Sé
Aszód
Tiszapolgár-Basatanya
Polgár
Sipenitsi
Miorcani
Draguşeni
Cucuteni
Vykhvatintsi
Petreni
Sabatinivka
Vladeni
Valeni
Valea Lupului
Vladimirivka
Varvarovka
Novye Ruseshty

TISZA CULTURE
Körös
Battonya
Vesztő-Mágor
Parta
Beletinci
Potporanj
Jela
Matejski Brod
Gomolava
Banica
BUTMIR
CULTURE
Nebo
Obre
Butmir
Vinča
Medvednjak
Rudna Glava
K'rameniti
Čuprija
Vinogradi
Drenovac
Svetozarevo
Radacje
VINCA
Fafos
Valač
Predionica
Gradac
CULTURE
Leskovica
Anza

Petreşti
Tartaria
Pianul de Jos
Turdaş
Vădăstra
Verbicioara
Farcaşu de Sus
Rast
Radaşeni
Brailiţa
Teiu
Vidra
Tangiru
Ruse
Hotnica
Gradešnica
Slatino
Azmak
Yasatepe
Ovčarovo
Kalojanovets
Karanovo
Sulica
Devetashka
Pazardžik
Berketskaja Mogila
Djadevo
Lovets

PETRESTI CULTURE
Ghēalešti-Nedeia
Izvoare
Buznea
Podei

Baia
HAMANGIA
CULTURE
Cernavoda
Sultana
Gulmeniţa
Varna
Goljamo Delčevo

KARANOVO CULTURE
Sitagroi

DANILO-HVAR CULTURE
nilčić
Hvar
Malik

Rakhmani
Žarkou
Dimini
DIMINI CULTURE
Corinth
Gonia
Asea

BLACK SEA

ANATOLIA

AEGEAN SEA

IONIAN SEA

ADRIATIC SEA

ITALY

In Southeast Europe between 5000 and 3000 BC, regional cultures developed with copper tools and painted and impressed (hand-marked) pottery. Many sites are known.

Two clay models, one of a cart (above), made in Hungary about 4000 BC, and one (below) from Romania, of four buildings, perhaps religious shrines or temples, on a base with holes. It is 51cm (20in) wide.

3 Crafts of Stone Age Europe

The Late Stone Age is sometimes called the 'Smooth-Stone Age', from the polished stone tools made by people at this time. This name is not entirely accurate, however, since polishing or smoothing stones for tools was done much earlier, as was the carving and smoothing of ivory and bone. As skills in toolmaking developed, so people spent more time mastering the skills, becoming specialist craftworkers. As well as stone arrowheads made with pointed tips and a notched end to fit into the wooden shaft, people also made short stone blades, either with or without saw-teeth. The large numbers of sickle-like tools show the growing importance of grain-harvesting.

The invention of pottery

The most important invention of the later Stone Age was undoubtedly pottery. Clay was shaped, smoothed and (most important) fired in heat to make all kinds of useful, liquid-holding containers.

People had earlier discovered how to shape wet clay to make objects and figures, some of which may have been hardened in fire. But it took time to discover that firing a clay pot made it harder and longer-lasting.

Pottery is first known from 6000 BC in western Syria, and around the same time in Anatolia, Turkey, and the Balkans. Evidence for the use of pottery by 5000 BC in the western Mediterranean region comes from many places, including sites in Italy, southern France and Spain.

Although the exact dates are not known, the appearance of this new technology in many places in Europe at

These objects of ceremonial and domestic use were found in burial mounds at Majkop in southern Russia, and date from about 2000 BC.

1 Silver vase with animal figure decoration. 2 Gold statuette of a bull. 3 and 4 Copper axe heads.

The pottery model (below), from about 3000 BC, of a building with a sloping roof, probably made from tree trunks is from Strelice, Moravia.

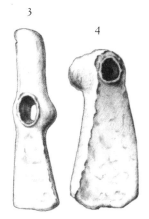

the same time suggests that pottery-making must have begun in several centres, and spread rapidly. Pottery-making extended from the Balkans to the west through Italy and France, and through Greece to the valley of the River Danube and the lands of central and north-west Europe. The knowledge was spread by trade and by contact across the sea as well as overland. Different regions developed their own forms of pottery.

The first farmers of Europe

Europe's first farmers lived in the Danube river basin and farming spread west through what are now the countries of Slovakia, the Czech Republic, Poland,

The houses in this farm village of Moldavia (pictured in colour on pages 12/13) were built in a ring around the largest and most important building – the temple.

The houses are rectangular with mud walls, strengthened inside by wooden poles and with sloping thatch roofs. There are small stone walls.

Most activities are linked to growing and harvesting cereals. Two farmers use long sticks to thresh the wheat harvested from the field and so separate the grain from the husks.

Much of the work is done by women. They pound the grain in large wooden mortars to make a coarse flour for daily use. By this time, other types of plants are cultivated as well as cereals, not all of them for food use. Women are busy stripping fibres from flax plants, to weave into linen cloth. Another woman is spinning.

Domestic animals roam about the village. There are dogs, oxen, pigs, sheep, goats and chickens.

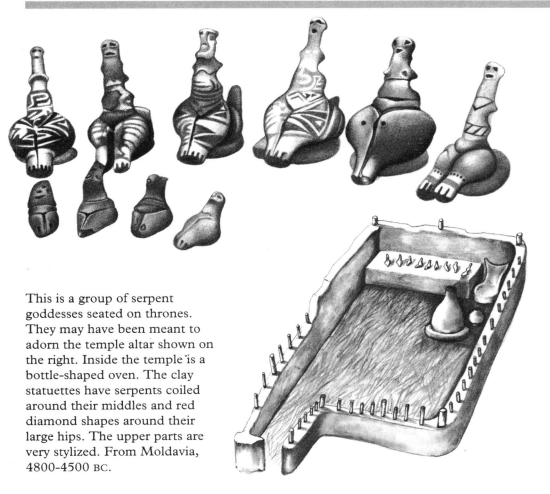

This is a group of serpent goddesses seated on thrones. They may have been meant to adorn the temple altar shown on the right. Inside the temple is a bottle-shaped oven. The clay statuettes have serpents coiled around their middles and red diamond shapes around their large hips. The upper parts are very stylized. From Moldavia, 4800-4500 BC.

Germany and the Netherlands. People grew cereals, especially wheat, on terraced hillsides and on plains spread with fertile soil deposited by flooding rivers. They reared cattle, pigs, sheep and goats. Their settlements were villages of large rectangular dwellings, all built to the same pattern but ranging in length from 6 to 45 metres (20 to 150ft).

Every village contained about ten buildings, and was home to between 50 and 170 people. They were probably wandering farmers who abandoned an area when the soil lost its fertility. This would explain their rapid spread north and west, but given the richness of the soil it is difficult to believe that farmers preferred to move from settled villages when sowing crops in rotation would have kept the land fertile.

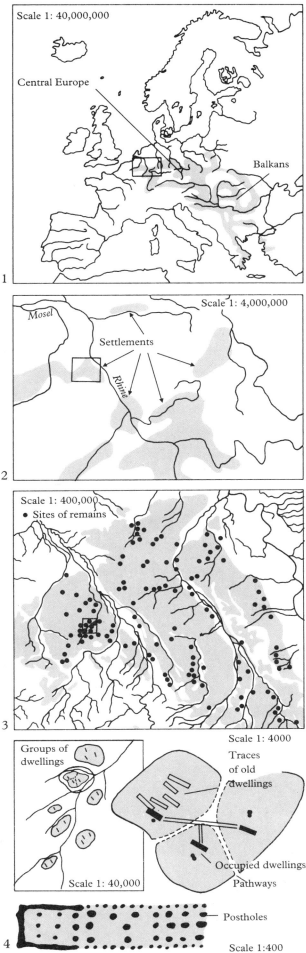

The map (1) shows Europe, around 5000-4000 BC. An area of western Germany (2) has been enlarged to show settlements in the Rhine Valley. A close-up of the boxed area (3) shows the density of sites along rivers in a smaller area. The diagram (4) shows typical features of a village site and the traces of buildings (such as postholes), revealed by modern archaeology.

15

The map shows settlements in Anatolia and Mesopotamia. In some of these towns and villages people had begun to make pottery and metal tools. Obsidian, a hard, volcanic mineral, was also traded for toolmaking.

Below is a plan of part of the town of Çatal Hüyük, reconstructed on the basis of the findings of archaeologists. The many temples (red) discovered so far seem no different on the outside from ordinary dwellings. In both buildings, the entrance was through the roof, by a stepladder connecting the different levels. The small windows made the inside dark, adding to the mysterious atmosphere when religious rites were performed.

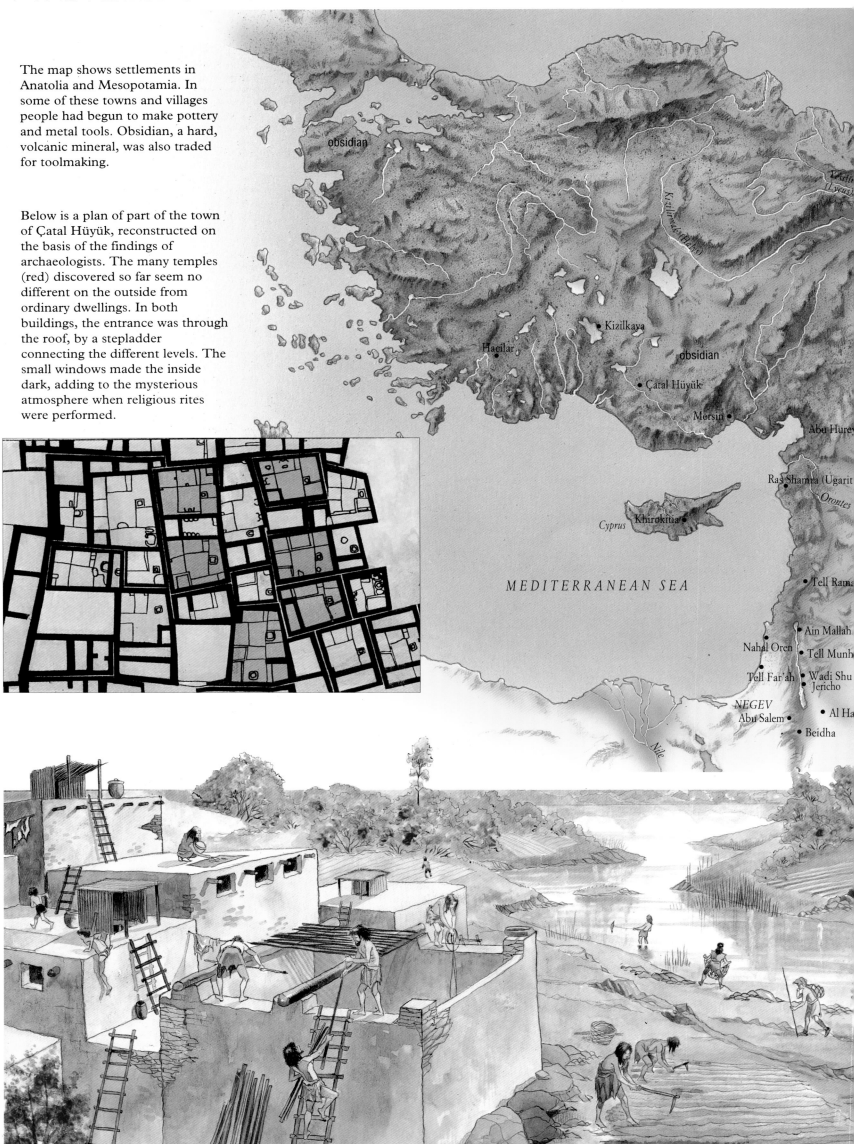

obsidian

Kizilkaya

Hacilar

obsidian

Çatal Hüyük

Mersin

Abu Hurey

Ras Shamra (Ugarit

Orontes

Cyprus   Khirokitia

MEDITERRANEAN SEA

Tell Rama

Ain Mallah

Nahal Oren   Tell Munh

Tell Far'ah   Wadi Shu
                Jericho

NEGEV
Abu Salem   Al Ha

Beidha

Nile

BLACK SEA

CAUCASUS

Kura

L.Sevan

Kura

Araks

obsidian

CASPIAN SEA

L.Van

L.Urmia

Zawi Chemi

Shanidar

bet

Qermez Dere

Halaf

Zarzi

Palegawra

Karim Shahir

IRANIAN DESERT

Jarmo

Bouqras

MESOPOTAMIA

Samarra

Tell es-Sawwan

Tepe Sarab

Tigris

Tepe Guran

SYRIAN DESERT

Ali Kosh

Euphrates

ARABIAN DESERT

The inset map shows sites where archaeologists have found evidence of the spread of domestic sheep and goats during the period before pottery was first made in this region (8500 to 7000 BC).

Ashikli Hüyük

L.Van

Cafer Hüyük

L.Urmia

Can Hasan

Tell Aswad

Nemrik

Mureybet

Ras Shamra
(Ugarit)

Euphrates

MESOPOTAMIA

Tigris

Jarmo

Cyprus

Tepe Guran

MEDITERRANEAN SEA

Ali Kosh

SYRIAN DESERT

Nahal Oren

NEGEV

ARABIAN DESERT

Nile

SINAI

17

4 THE FERTILE CRESCENT FROM STONE AGE TO COPPER AGE

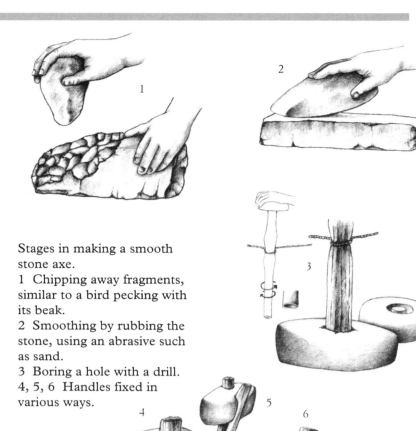

Stages in making a smooth stone axe.
1 Chipping away fragments, similar to a bird pecking with its beak.
2 Smoothing by rubbing the stone, using an abrasive such as sand.
3 Boring a hole with a drill.
4, 5, 6 Handles fixed in various ways.

In the Middle East from around 7000 BC a process of change began that was to alter human life radically. The Fertile Crescent (see pages 10-11) was already occupied by settled farmers, and the village was the centre of their lives. Settlements such as Samarra and Tell es-Sawwan on the River Tigris, Halaf on a tributary of the River Euphrates, Hacilar in Turkey and others in the Palestine region were founded on the sites of earlier settlements of hunter-gatherers. The people who lived in such settlements differed from the earlier occupants by building more solid houses of bricks and mud, with whitewashed walls and floors. Their villages were more compact, and they practised a form of farming that made use of irrigation systems, allowing even arid areas to be cultivated.

The town of Çatal Hüyük
In the same period, on the plains of Konya in south-central Anatolia (modern Turkey), the town of Çatal Hüyük reached an exceptional level of culture. For about a thousand years from 6200 BC, this settlement was not a simple village but a real town. Sited in an area well supplied with river water, Çatal Hüyük covered 32 hectares (nearly 80 acres). It had a thousand houses and a population of between 5000 and 6000 people.

This outstanding town exercised economic influence, and almost certainly political control, over surrounding areas. Other than the usual cereals and vegetables, the people of Çatal Hüyük grew rape, and harvested quantities of almonds and pistachio nuts. They also hunted wild cattle, donkeys and ibex. Dogs and sheep were their only domestic animals.

The inhabitants of Çatal Hüyük were not just farmers, however. Their houses and burial places have revealed rich examples of craftsmanship and art, including wall-paintings and sculptures. Increased trade with distant regions enabled the craftworkers to beautify their work. For example, silicon came from Syria, obsidian from Armenia. Marble and malachite, turquoise and copper, used for decoration and ornaments, also came from afar.

The beginnings of metalworking
In the 7000s BC in Anatolia, Mesopotamia, Armenia

On the borders of the plains of Konya in south-central Turkey, the inhabitants of Çatal Hüyük (pictured in colour on pages 16/17) are shown building more houses on the outskirts of their town.

It is already an important centre. The houses are rectangular, made of dried bricks, and in rows. There are no roads. Access to a house is by ladder through the roof, and because the houses are on different levels the small windows at the top look out on the roof below. This makes the town a complex and close-knit centre, with no need for further defences such as walls.

In the fields nearby, farmers cultivate barley, corn, vegetables and rape. The river is close enough to make irrigation simple, and also provides fishing with harpoons and nets. Successful hunters return with a gazelle; others have more difficulty trying to capture a wild ox.

Life for the woman milking her sheep seems easier than for the gatherers, trudging home from the forest with food and firewood.

A cutaway reconstruction (top right) of one of the many temples at Çatal Hüyük, discovered between 1961 and 1963 by the British archaeologist James Mellaart. Skulls of bulls and rams (symbols of male divinity) are nailed on the crude brick walls and on the seats. The walls are decorated with reliefs and paintings. The centrepiece is a large relief of a 'mother-goddess' giving birth. The dead were buried under the floor, where there is also a hearth.

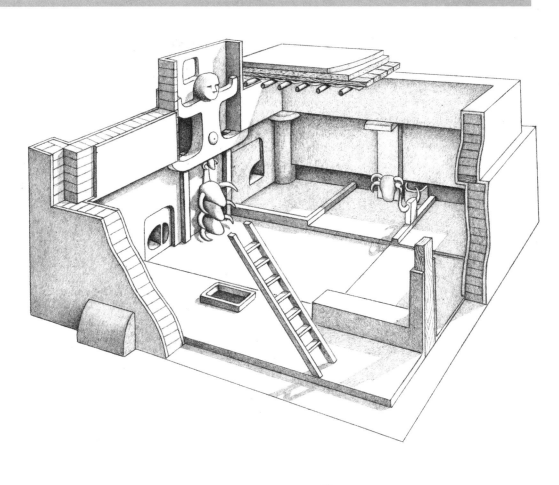

The houses of Çatal Hüyük (right centre) were no different in structure from the temples, and were entered from the roof by ladder. Each dwelling, which was usually about 25 metres square (270sq ft), presumably housed one family, and was built of bricks on a wooden frame. The hearth was dug out from the floor, and in the wall was an oven, with a flue to the outside.

Pictures (bottom right) of a vulture and of a headless human are from a temple wall. Bodies were beheaded before burial.

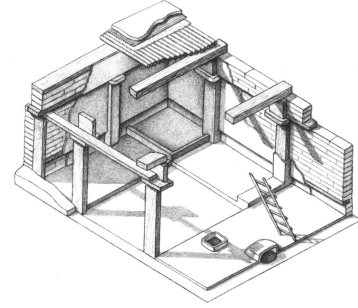

and around the Caucasus Mountains, people had found metals such as copper and gold in their natural state, as grains or as lumps mixed with other minerals. Craft-workers and artists were attracted by their colour but also by the flexibility of these soft metals, which could be worked into many shapes. Copper and gold were cold-hammered and cut to make necklaces. These early examples can not yet be called metalwork, but by 3000 BC people had begun to heat copper, which made it much more flexible and easier to work.

This next stage towards true metalworking came with the use of primitive smelting – separating the mineral from its ore by heating it to temperatures as high as 700°C – the same temperature required to fire clay pots. So the experience gained of using heat in pottery influenced the new metalworking techniques. In Anatolia, by the 3000s BC, metalworkers were smelting copper in kilns using bellows to raise the temperature inside to over 1000°C. The liquid metal was then poured into stone moulds or sand casts, and by this simple procedure, the first metalworkers were able to create a required shape (such as a sword blade) and produce others of the same shape.

Society and commerce develop

Metalworkers and potters specialized more and more. They exchanged their goods and skills for food produced by farmers. In this way society became more complex, and so did relations between one community and its neighbours. Stone tools were giving way to copper tools, giving this culture the name 'Chalcolithic' (from the Greek *chalkos*, 'copper', and *lithos*, 'stone'). Copper-using cultures spread and became increasingly diverse.

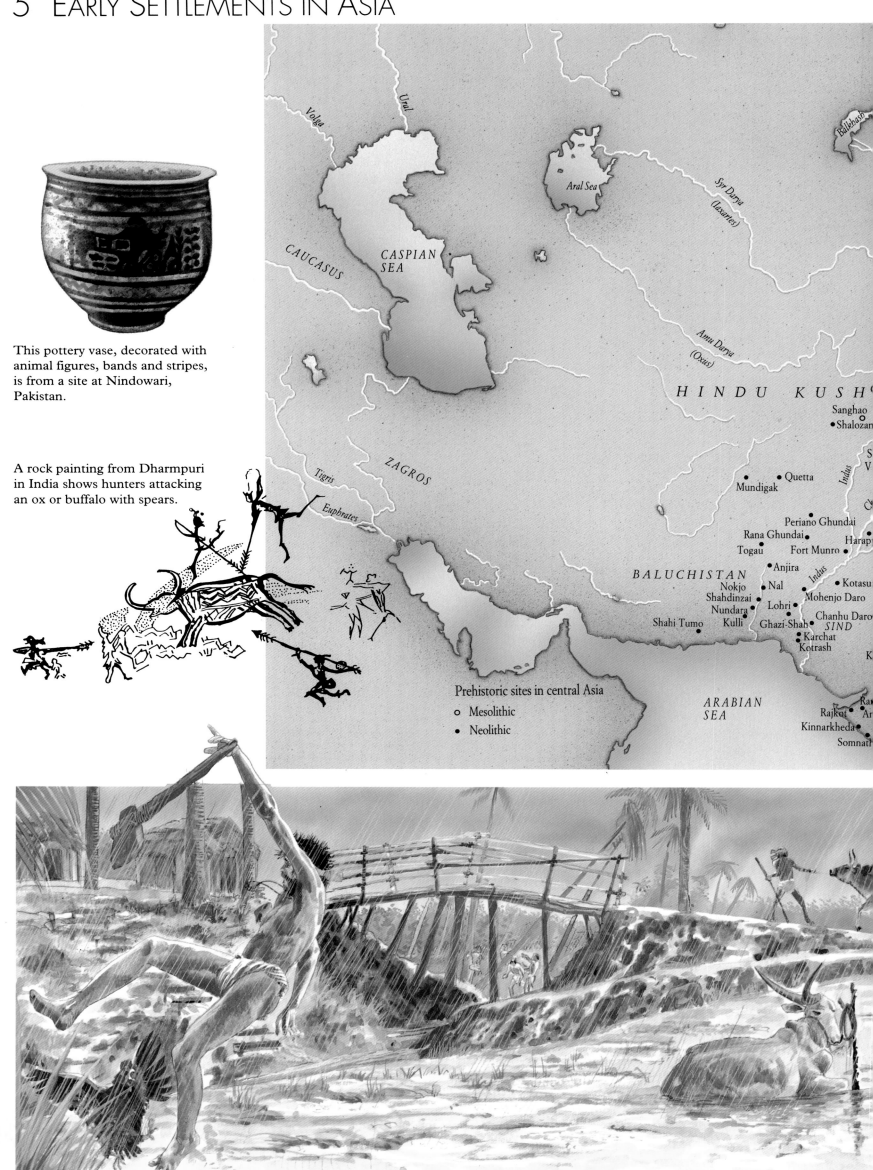

This pottery vase, decorated with animal figures, bands and stripes, is from a site at Nindowari, Pakistan.

A rock painting from Dharmpuri in India shows hunters attacking an ox or buffalo with spears.

Prehistoric sites in central Asia
○ Mesolithic
● Neolithic

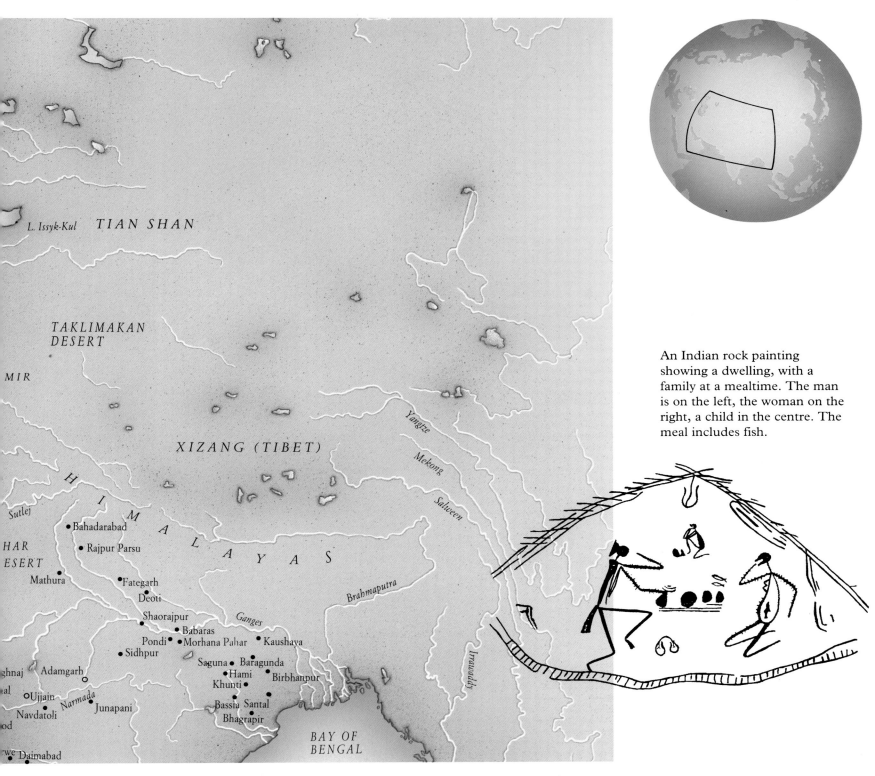

TIAN SHAN

L. Issyk-Kul

TAKLIMAKAN
DESERT

MIR

XIZANG (TIBET)

Yangtze

Mekong

Salween

Sutlej

H
I
M
A
L
A
Y
A
S

HAR
ESERT

Bahadarabad

Rajpur Parsu

Mathura

Fategarh

Deoti

Brahmaputra

Shaorajpur

Ganges

Babaras

Pondi

Morhana Pahar

Kaushaya

Sidhpur

Saguna

Baragunda

Hami

Birbhanpur

Khunti

ghnaj

Adamgarh

Bassia

Santal

al

Ujjain

Narmada

Junapani

Bhagrapir

Irrawaddy

Navdatoli

od

BAY OF
BENGAL

we Daimabad

An Indian rock painting showing a dwelling, with a family at a mealtime. The man is on the left, the woman on the right, a child in the centre. The meal includes fish.

5 EARLY SETTLEMENTS IN ASIA

From about 7000 BC small groups of wandering peoples carried the new ways of farming east from the Fertile Crescent across the Zagros Mountains into Iran and the Indian sub-continent, and also north across the Caucasus Mountains into central Asia.

Farmers, potters and traders

These people lived in simple villages of rectangular houses, gathering and growing various kinds of wild cereals. They also bred goats, as well as hunting wild animals.

They made rough pottery, which was fired at low temperatures and so was not very hard-wearing. But distinctive painted pottery developed in various places. Where they found rich mineral deposits, people began trading in gemstones and copper. Such exchanges of goods established regular links between the towns of the Fertile Crescent and the newer settlements founded between the Black Sea and the Caspian Sea, and in the river valleys of what is now Iran.

Copper-working and irrigation

By 4000 BC people in Iran were smelting copper and founding towns, despite the difficulties of desert and mountain terrain. In isolated towns such as Tepe Yahya (southern Iran) people produced copper, which was exchanged for salt and farm produce from the farmers living on the more thickly populated and fertile plains.

In dry areas, farmers practised irrigation. A good example of this is the Djeitun culture (just east of the

Methods of making pottery.
1 Modelling a bowl by hand.
2 Flattening a plate shape.
3 Using a small rush basket as a mould.
4 Coiling a long 'sausage' of clay.

Caspian Sea), where archaeologists have found remains of villages of scattered one-room houses, with ovens.

Farmers in the Indian sub-continent

Before 4000 BC there were farmers in northern India, around the Indus River. The first farm settlements were scattered groups of houses with reed walls covered in mud. Goats and sheep were kept, and the people also gathered wild cereals, fished and hunted. They began

This village in northwest India (pictured in colour on pages 20/21) is built alongside a river. The seasonal monsoon rains, shown in full force, were vital to the life of this whole region – as they still are.

The houses are rectangular, with straw thatch roofs and reed walls plastered with mud.

During the rains, daily life is carried on in the shelter of the overhanging roofs – though some villagers have to venture out, perhaps to catch a chicken for supper. Women cook food, make and paint pottery, and make cloth.

The men use stone stools to cut timber and bamboo to make a bridge over the irrigation ditches dug by everyone in the village to water the fields. A tame ox hauls a heavy log. Other domestic animals roam freely around the houses. People keep chickens, pigs and cattle. The animal dung is dried and used as fuel for fires.

An early version of
the potter's wheel,
turned by hand.

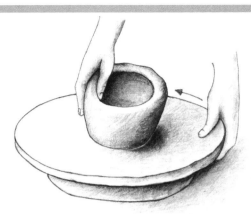

Below are five methods of decorating pottery.
1 Scratching a pattern with a finger or fingernail.
2 Indenting the clay with a shell ('cardial').
3 Combing the clay with a bone tool.
4 Pressing a coiled cord into the clay ('corded').
5 Using a spatula to smooth the clay and an awl
  to make swirls in it.

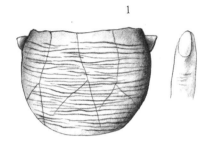

Section of a
potter's wheel.

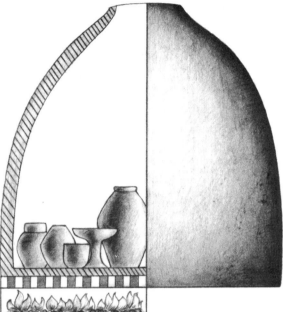

A potter's kiln (left) cut away to show
pots of various shapes. The heat could
circulate evenly and such kilns could
reach temperatures high enough to
fire clay containing iron and
manganese, which gave the pots a
white, red and black colour.

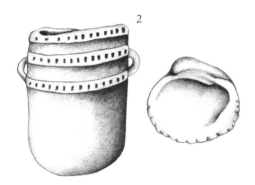

planting crops on land which had been cleared by
'slashing and burning' the wild forest. Rice was already
being grown in the valley of the River Ganges.

The people also began to make crude pottery and
copper tools, and to domesticate new animals such as
pigs and cattle. The new farmers were prevented from
expanding northwards by the high mountains of the
Hindu Kush and Himalaya, but founded new settlements in the Punjab region of northern India. They
then moved out onto the plains, mastering improved
forms of crop-irrigation.

Most settlements were simple villages. An exception
is Mundigak in Afghanistan. Here archaeologists have
found the remains of an imposing town with walls and a
palace or temple, dating from before 3000 BC. Such settlements preceded the rise of the great civilization of the
Indus Valley (Harappa and Mohenjo-Daro) a few centuries later.

Steppe farmers and herders
To the north of India people living on the vast plains or
steppes of central Asia started to domesticate animals
and, very gradually, to grow and harvest crops. Farming
proper, however, came much later, at the same time as
permanent settlements consisting of pit-dwellings. For
reasons unknown, these villages were soon abandoned
and the peoples of the steppes became horse-riding
nomads, herding animals such as sheep and camels
rather than planting crops.

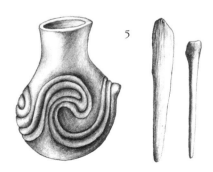

The main map shows late Stone Age and Bronze Age sites in China.

A Chinese ritual vase from about 1000 BC, made in bronze, with a water buffalo motif.

The inset map (on page 25) shows Shang civilization sites. The dark yellow shows the origins of Shang culture (from about 1800 BC), the paler yellow its spread across China.

This picture from the Yinshan Mountains of Inner Mongolia shows a tiger, with goat kids.

Uzbel Pass

TARIM PENDI

TAKLIMAKAN DESERT

Tarim He

L. Lop Nur

Khunjerab Pass

BADAIN JARAN SHAMO

X I N J I A N G

K2

KUNLUN SHAN

Karakoram Pass

GANS

QAIDAM PENDI

L. Qing

X I Z A N G

(T I B E T)

QINGHAI

Mach

KASHMIR

Dhaulagiri

Annapurna

H I M A L A Y A

Everest

Ganges

Brahmaputra

Haimenkou

I N D I A

Shijia

BANGLADESH

BURMA

Ganges delta

Irrawaddy

Salween

Mekong

BAY OF BENGAL

I N D O C H I N A

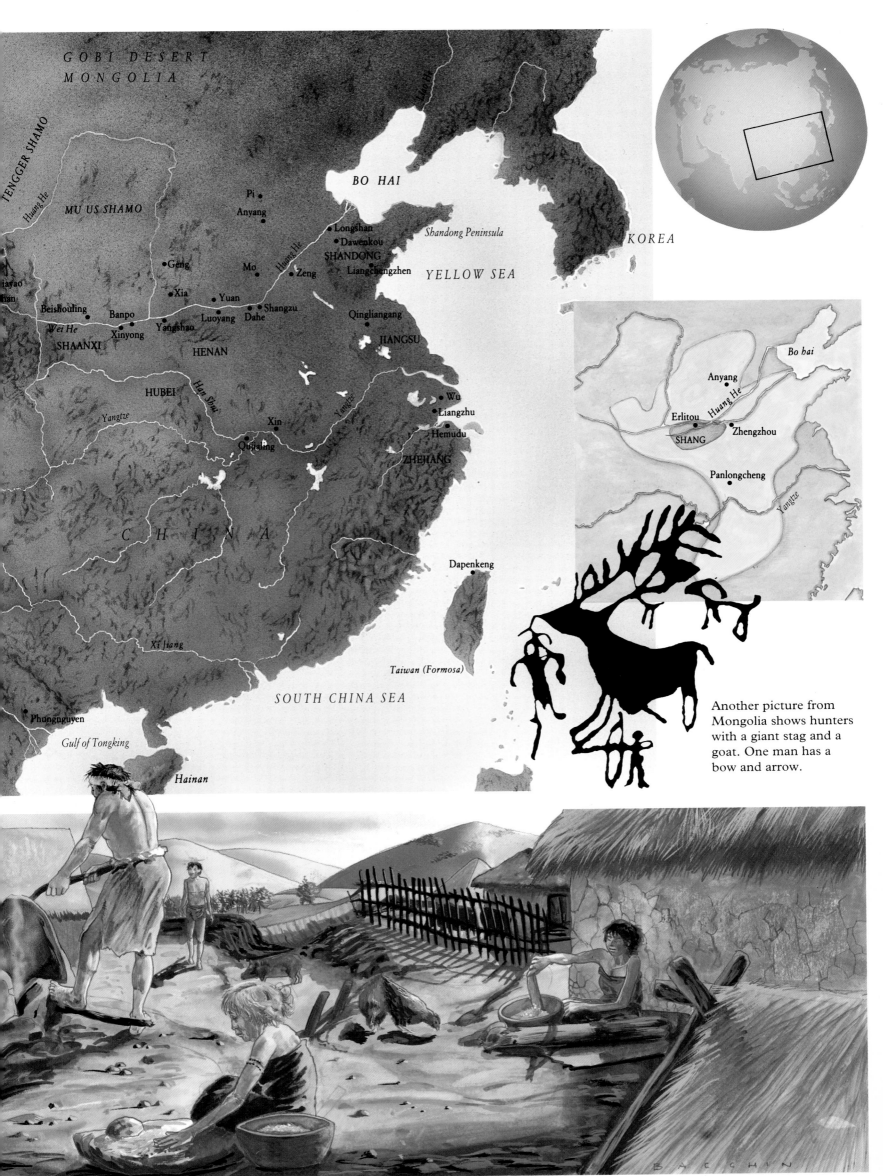

GOBI DESERT
MONGOLIA

TENGGER SHAMO

MU US SHAMO

Huang He

Pi

Anyang

BO HAI

Longshan
Dawenkou
SHANDONG
Liangchengzhen

Shandong Peninsula

KOREA

YELLOW SEA

Geng

Mo

Huang He

Zeng

Xia

Yuan

Beishouling

Banpo

Shangzu

Luoyang Dahe

Xinyong Yangshao

Wei He

SHAANXI

HENAN

Qingliangang

JIANGSU

HUBEI

Han Shui

Yangtze

Wu

Liangzhu

Xin

Hemudu

Yangtze

Quijiang

ZHEJIANG

C H I N A

Dapenkeng

Xi Jiang

Taiwan (Formosa)

Phungnguyen

SOUTH CHINA SEA

Gulf of Tongking

Hainan

Bo hai

Anyang

Erlitou Huang He

SHANG Zhengzhou

Panlongcheng

Yangtze

Another picture from
Mongolia shows hunters
with a giant stag and a
goat. One man has a
bow and arrow.

25

6 THE FIRST FARMERS OF CHINA

Little is known about human settlement in China during the period of the Stone Age before farming began. Archaeologists think that there was a long period of Stone Age life in south China, with the making of pebble tools, hunting of animals (leading to gradual domestication of some species), food-gathering and especially fishing along the rivers and sea coasts, where the human population was quite dense.

River communities

The first farming communities appeared, not by chance, in the temperate lands of north China, along two great rivers, the Huang He, or Yellow River, and the Yangtze. There the soil was fertile and easy to cultivate, even for people with primitive tools.

Although this region was more exposed than the south to outside influences (from the Middle East, India and northern Asia), the first farming communities in China were actually the result of an evolution that came about in China itself. From about 4000 BC this produced a culture known as Yangshao, after a village in Henan province where remains of hundreds of stone tools have been found.

Farmers on the move

The Yangshao farmers grew cereals, including millet and wheat, which could survive long dry periods. These formed the mainstay of their diet, alongside plants and seeds gathered in the wild. They also hunted wild oxen, deer and horses. The farmers reared pigs and dogs for food. Fishing was also important.

A bone ploughshare, from about 4000 BC.

A hoe or spade made from the shoulder-blade of an ox.

Stone axes, found in south China, from about 3000-2000 BC.

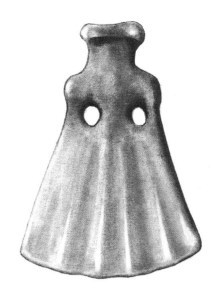

These Stone Age farmers practised a nomadic agriculture known as 'slash and burn'. Forested areas were burned and cleared for planting, the ash enriching the soil and producing good harvests. But when the soil was exhausted, the farmers had to move on and clear new patches of forest. Rather than living in settled farms, the Yangshao people moved on every few years.

This Chinese village (pictured in colour on pages 24/25) would have been one of many small settlements in the temperate north, often only 10km (6 miles) apart. The round or box-shaped houses have straw roofs and mud walls. Around the village is a ditch, giving some protection against wild animals and hostile neighbours.

Some children greet a fisherman returning in his boat. The village women look after the animals (pigs, dogs and chickens) or sort and grind the grain. Two men are making clay pots, carefully seeing to the last stages of firing: the walls of the kiln are broken open and they scatter sand and earth onto the ashes to cool the pots.

This clay bowl, decorated with stylized fish, is from the Yangshao culture, around 4000 BC.

This amphora, or storage jar, with spiral decoration, is also from the Yangshao period.

This tripod jug is from the later Longshan period.

This picture of ritual dancers, with raised arms and legs spread apart, is from a rock painting in Guangxi province, China.

A typical village

At the Banpo settlement on the Huang He, 46 houses have been discovered. They give a fairly clear picture of how the people lived. The villages had many houses, with about 200 inhabitants, apparently living without any well-defined social hierarchy. The houses were round, with tar and straw roofs, held up by stout vertical poles. Inside, in the centre of the floor, was a hearth for fires. Around the house was a ditch. The making of pottery played an important part in this and later Chinese civilizations.

A more advanced society

The first signs of a more complex society come from Longshan. At this site archaeologists have found evidence of a later farming culture (from about 3000 BC). This had much in common with Yangshao, but the villages seem to have been permanent. They were protected by earth barricades, suggesting that the people now practised a more settled form of farming.

Millet was still the staple food, but rice was also grown, having reached China from Southeast Asia, where it was already important. Sheep, horses, oxen and water buffalo were all reared, as well as pigs and dogs.

From around 2500 BC, growing differences in burial practices marked a gradual evolution towards a more hierarchical society, possibly with priests. Tribal settlements spread along the Huang He, and evidence of bronze objects suggests that metalworking began after 2000 BC.

Below are reconstructions of two dwellings, from finds made at Banpo. Round houses, 3.5 metres (11.5ft) across, were probably home to just one family. The larger rectangular type of dwelling, measuring 11 by 10 metres (36 by 32ft), would have been used by a family clan or group of families.

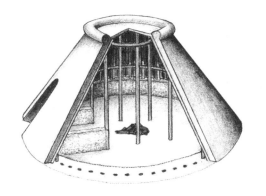

The main map shows sites of the Jomon and Yayoi cultures. Inset far left is a map of Japan as it was during the last Ice Age (20,000 years ago) when it was still connected to the mainland of Asia and partly covered by ice. Inset left is a map of the Japanese islands separated from the rest of Asia about 10,000 BC.

CHINA

SEA OF JAPAN

HOKKAIDO

KOREA

HONSHU

SHIKOKU

KYUSHU

PACIFIC OCEAN

▲Jomon
○Yayoi

SEA OF JAPAN

○Dogahama
▲Sempukuji
Itatsuke
▲Fukui
○○ Mikumo
Ankokuji
Sozudai ▲ ○
KYUSHU
▲Kamikuroiwa
SHIKOKU

Mizukamidani ▲ ▲Fudodo
▲Torihama
Tenjinyama ○ ○●Kitashirakawa
Ama ○ HONSH
Uriyudo ○

Togariishi ▲ ▲Idojiri
▲Yosukeone
Daima
Toro ○ Otsuka ○
Natsushima ▲ K
K

PACIFIC OCEAN

▲Nishihara

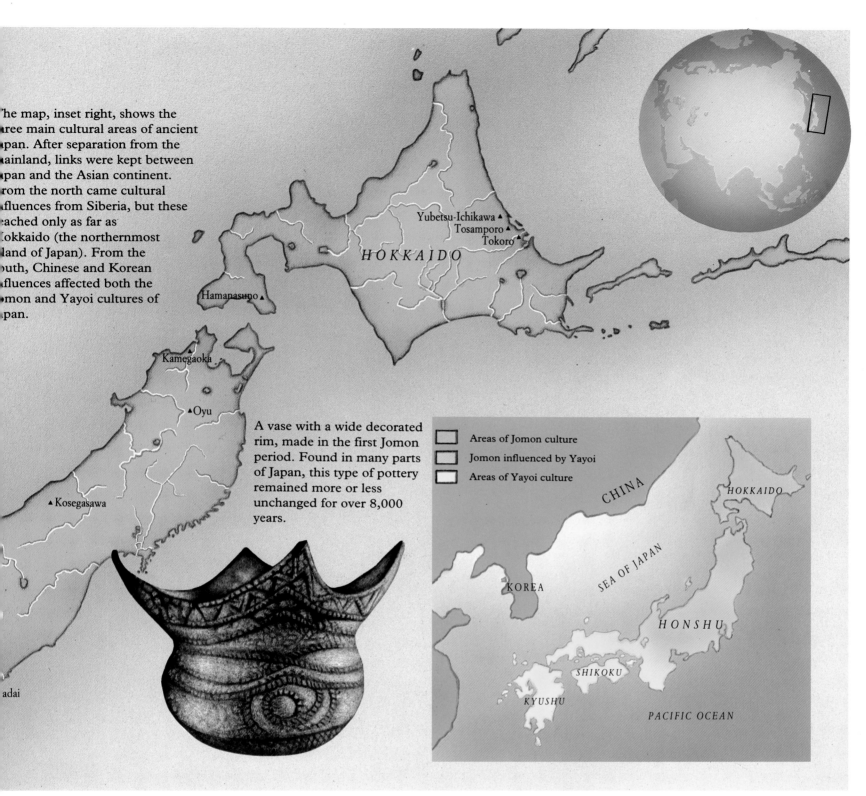

The map, inset right, shows the three main cultural areas of ancient Japan. After separation from the mainland, links were kept between Japan and the Asian continent. From the north came cultural influences from Siberia, but these reached only as far as Hokkaido (the northernmost island of Japan). From the south, Chinese and Korean influences affected both the Jomon and Yayoi cultures of Japan.

Yubetsu-Ichikawa ▲
Tosamporo ▲
Tokoro ▲

HOKKAIDO

▲ Hamanasuno

▲ Kamegaoka

▲ Oyu

▲ Kosegasawa

adai

A vase with a wide decorated rim, made in the first Jomon period. Found in many parts of Japan, this type of pottery remained more or less unchanged for over 8,000 years.

☐ Areas of Jomon culture
☐ Jomon influenced by Yayoi
☐ Areas of Yayoi culture

CHINA

HOKKAIDO

KOREA

SEA OF JAPAN

HONSHU

SHIKOKU

KYUSHU

PACIFIC OCEAN

7 ANCIENT JAPAN

Japan is a mountainous country. Only part of the land was suitable for farming even after widespread clearance by 'slash and burn'. As well as being scarce, land fit for cultivation was also very scattered, separated by the barren mountains.

The first hunters and fishers

Traces of the first human settlements date from more than 14,000 years ago, when hunters from mainland Asia arrived by the 'land bridge' still joining it to Japan. These settlements were isolated groups of villages, where people lived by hunting and fishing. The sea coasts had probably always been picked over for oysters, clams and other shellfish, and enormous deposits of shells (known as shell middens) have been found. But the warmer sea temperature at the end of the Ice Age greatly increased fishing. Hooks and harpoons made of horn or bone, and fishing nets, show how important the sea was as a food source.

The remains of large sea fish such as tuna, ray and shark found in the shell middens show that fishing was also done in deep waters. This suggests that the men were away for long periods, while their families stayed at home growing small crops of cereals (barley and oats), and picking wild plants such as couch grass and bamboo shoots, as well as walnuts, acorns and chestnuts.

Village life

Deer and wild boar were hunted for meat, as were smaller animals. Dogs were also probably reared for eating. The chief hunting weapons were bows and arrows tipped with double-edged heads of bone or stone.

Because of the lack of farmland, the few villages were small, with seldom more than 15 dwellings. They were

Roughly midway through the Jomon period, people began to bury the dead in large shell middens. These heaps did not wear away and so gave lasting protection to the bodies. People also began to make clay figures of goddesses and disc-shaped masks of human faces with large protruding eyes.

This clay mask with face markings that make it appear to wink is from the late Jomon period.

This terracotta figure, also late Jomon, is possibly to do with a fertility cult.

loose-knit communities with no evidence of hierarchy or social classes.

The modest houses were rectangular, round or trapezoid in shape and simply made. They had sunken floors, so a person could stand upright even though the building was low. The sloping roof was usually made of tree bark, reeds or woven branches, and reached right down to the ground, without walls. The roof was propped up by wooden poles and cross bars.

Jomon Japan

In open kilns people fired a type of pottery decorated with markings made by a cord or rope. This pottery came to be called Jomon, after the site where it was first found in the shell middens of Omori near Tokyo. It remained in use for thousands of years in a rich variety of styles that evolved with time and usage.

The Jomon people buried their dead simply, in

The left-hand picture (shown in colour on page 28) is of a Jomon village, close to the shore and an active volcano – a constant threat in Japan. Shellfish such as oysters, mussels and clams were gathered in enormous quantities for food. Their shells formed enormous middens around

every village.

The villagers were hunters and fishers. Farming was limited to small crops of wild wheat and millet. The shortage of pasture discouraged animal-rearing, though the people did keep pigs and dogs for meat.

The right-hand picture (shown in colour on page 29) is of a settlement of the later Yayoi period on the coast of Kyushu Island. The houses have sloping roofs and each has a ditch around it. A dirt bank and a fence surround the village. The little bridges are made of

bamboo. The villagers are skilled fishermen. They also grow barley and rice (which needs a flooded field). Women plant the rice, while an old woman grinds grain in a mortar. A man is working on the handle-fixing of a stone tool.

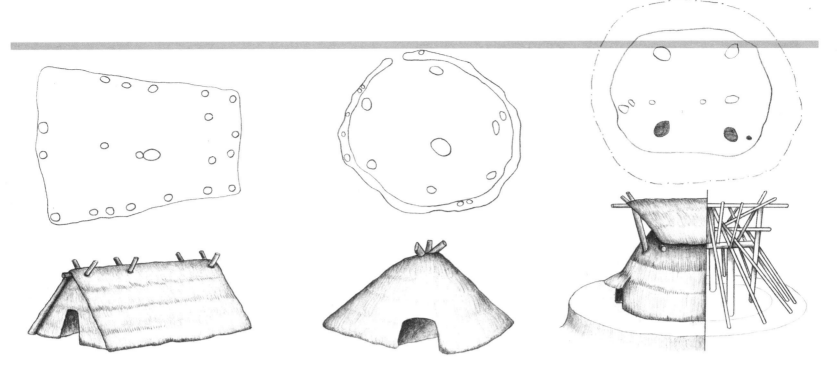

There were two basic shapes of pit huts made in the Jomon period. Both had steeply sloped roofs to ground level, which meant that there was no need for walls. The buildings were supported by frames of interlaced poles. You can see the position of the poles in the 'ground plans' above each house. The hearth was in the middle.

The houses of the later Yayoi period also had straw roofs that acted as walls. The building required a light but very complicated framework of wooden supports, shown in the cutaway section. A ditch surrounded the house.

crouching or stretched-out positions, sometimes under stones. The only monuments are from about 2000 BC, and most are in the northern part of the islands of Hokkaido and Honshu. They are arrangements of stones, placed side by side and upright, in uniform patterns and enclosed by a fence. Stylized figures of goddesses appeared midway through the 2000s BC.

During the last Jomon period (about 300 BC), barley- and rice-growing spread to Japan from Korea. Rice, which had been grown in small amounts for more than a thousand years, became the staple food in Japan. So began a new phase of culture, called Yayoi, from the district in Tokyo where the first remains were found.

Yayoi Japan

During this time people in western Japan lived mainly by farming, apart from in the northern island of Hokkaido, where, because of the cold climate, farming was not possible. That rice was grown is shown by traces of rice-fields and irrigation channels, and by finds of flaked-stone reaping-knives, and wooden farm tools such as hoes, spades and rakes. Animal-rearing played little part in Japanese life, as enough meat could be obtained by hunting and fishing.

Houses were more spacious and solid, but still had the Jomon characteristics. One new feature was the communal barn, built to accommodate the great increase in cereal production, which yielded larger and more reliable food stores. This abundance favoured the division of labour (different people doing different tasks) and the adoption of new technological processes, learned from China and Korea. The potter's wheel was introduced, as well as bronze-working, although at first this was limited to making ritual objects such as bells without clappers – which seem to have been a sign of prosperity. Tomb evidence shows that there was still little development of social rank or status. Ruling families emerged later.

The bronze bell without a clapper, called a *dotaku*, is one of the most characteristic ritual objects of central Japan in the Yayoi period. It is shown below surrounded by bronze weapons – spear points, a dagger, and a large halberd. Weapons too large to be used easily possibly served as a sign of the owner's importance. Bronze-working came later in the Yayoi period (early centuries AD).

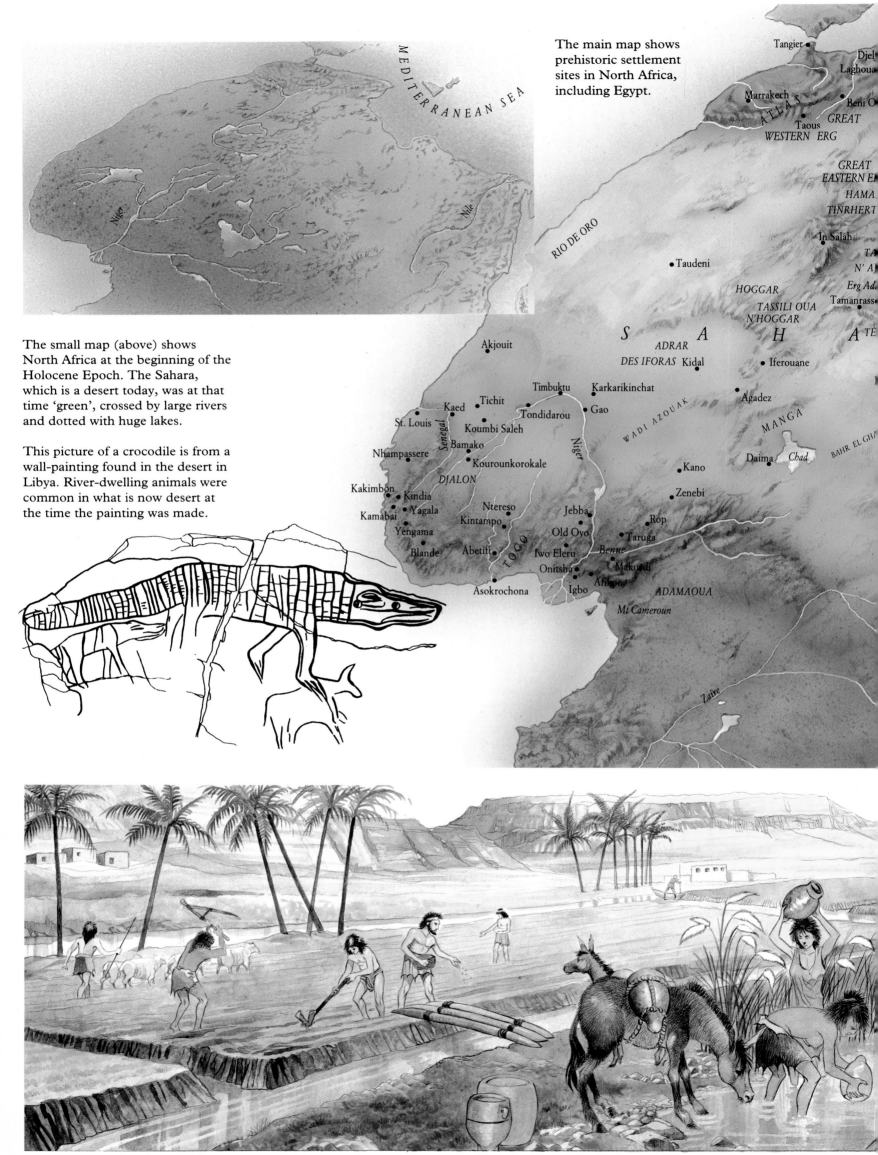

The main map shows prehistoric settlement sites in North Africa, including Egypt.

The small map (above) shows North Africa at the beginning of the Holocene Epoch. The Sahara, which is a desert today, was at that time 'green', crossed by large rivers and dotted with huge lakes.

This picture of a crocodile is from a wall-painting found in the desert in Libya. River-dwelling animals were common in what is now desert at the time the painting was made.

MEDITERRANEAN SEA

Niger

Nile

Tangier

Djel
Laghoua

Marrakech
ATLAS
GREAT
Taous
WESTERN ERG

GREAT
EASTERN E
HAMA
TINRHERT

RIO DE ORO

In Salah

Beni O

Taudeni

TA
N' A
Erg Ad

HOGGAR
TASSILI OUA
N'HOGGAR

Tamanrass

TÉ

Akjouit

S   A   H   A

ADRAR
DES IFORAS   Kidal

Iferouane

Timbuktu   Karkarikinchat

Kaed   Tichit   Gao

Agadez

St. Louis   Tondidarou

Koumbi Saleh

WADI AZOUAK

MANGA

Nhampassere   Bamako

Senegal   Kourounkorokale

Niger

Daima   Chad

BAHR EL GHA

Kano

Kakimbon

DJALON   Kindia

Ntereso

Zenebi

Kamabai   Yagala

Kintampo

Jebba

Rop

Yengama

Old Oyo

Taruga

Blande   Abetift

Iwo Eleru   Benue   Makurdi

TOGO   Onitsha   Igbo   Afikpo

Asokrochona

ADAMAOUA

Mt Cameroun

Zaire

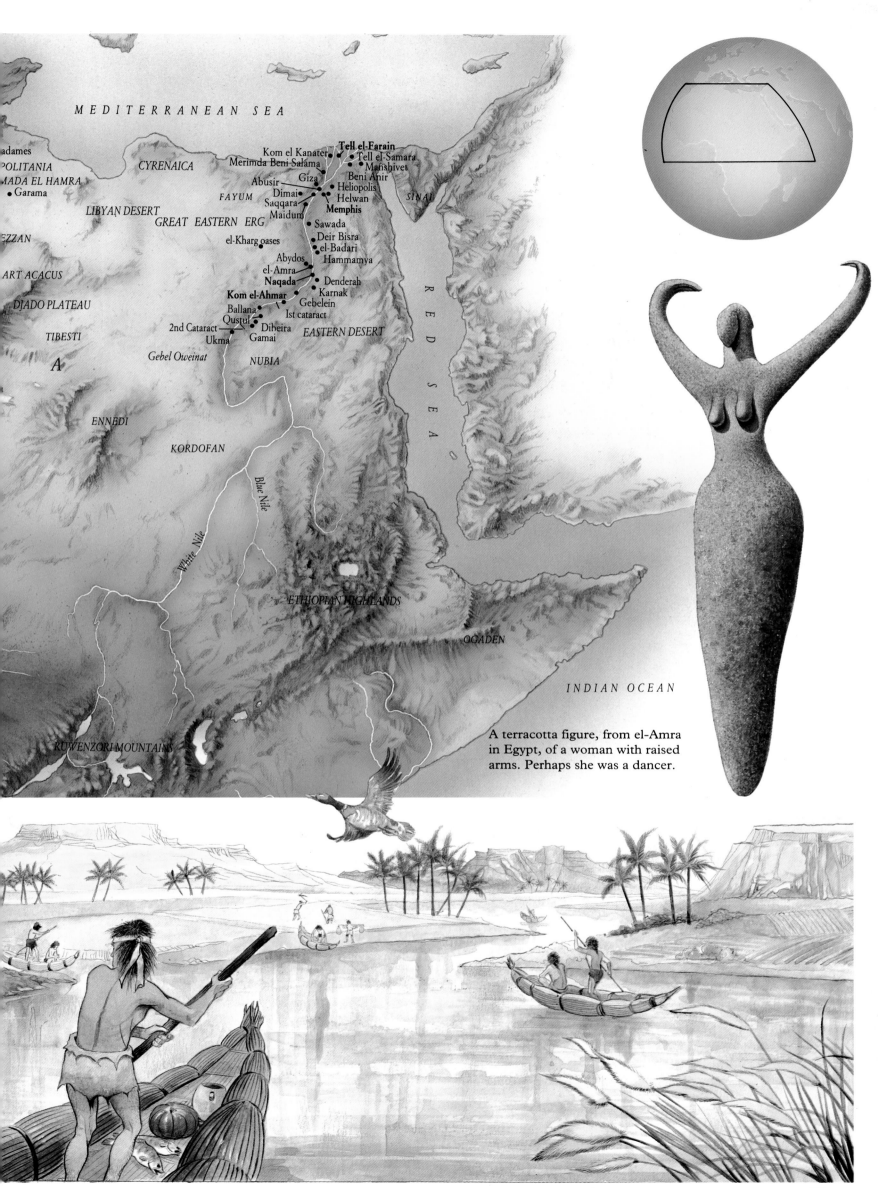

MEDITERRANEAN SEA

CYRENAICA

POLITANIA

MADA EL HAMRA

• Garama

LIBYAN DESERT

FAYUM

GREAT EASTERN ERG

EZZAN

ART ACACUS

DJADO PLATEAU

TIBESTI

A

ENNEDI

KORDOFAN

Blue Nile

White Nile

ETHIOPIAN HIGHLANDS

OGADEN

RUWENZORI MOUNTAINS

Kom el Kanater
Merimda Beni-Salama
Tell el-Farain
• Tell el-Samara
• Manshivet
Abusir
Giza
Beni Anir
Dimai
Heliopolis
Saqqara
Helwan
Maidum
Memphis
Sawada
Deir Bisra
el-Kharg oases
el-Badari
Hammamya
Abydos
el-Amra
Naqada
Denderah
Kom el-Ahmar
Karnak
Ballana
Gebelein
Qustul
1st cataract
2nd Cataract
Diheira
Ukma
Gamai
Gebel Oweinat
NUBIA

SINAI

RED SEA

EASTERN DESERT

INDIAN OCEAN

A terracotta figure, from el-Amra
in Egypt, of a woman with raised
arms. Perhaps she was a dancer.

8 The 'Green Sahara' and Early Egypt

At the end of the last Ice Age, around 10,000 years ago, the warming in the earth's temperature made the climate of North Africa much more moist. Monsoon rains gave rise to the 'greening' of what is now the Sahara.

A land of lakes and rivers

The Sahara became a region of lakes and rivers (see the small map on page 32). Land that is now sand-covered was filled by huge lakes, fed by rivers branching out in all directions. Highlands such as the Hoggar and Tibesti mountains were particularly green and fertile. In regions now arid such as Ténéré (Land of Fear) in Niger, people lived beside lakes full of fish, as we know from finds of harpoons, fishing hooks and arrowheads. These people knew how to make stone axes and sculptures of animals in basalt (hard, volcanic rock).

In the mountains the damp climate produced a spurt of vegetation, with oak, walnut, lime and alder trees. At lower altitudes, pine, juniper, willow and olive trees flourished. These are all trees now more associated with the Mediterranean region. The vast grassy plains were home to a variety of wildlife, including gazelle, antelope, elephant and buffalo; and in the lakes and rivers there were hippos, crocodiles and many kinds of fish.

Civilizations of the Sahara

The favourable climate made it possible for people to move into the Sahara and start settlements. These were similar to those in the Fertile Crescent of the Middle East, but had the great advantage of the huge supplies of Saharan water. The laborious constructions of canals like those dug by people in Mesopotamia was not needed.

One of the oldest sites is Amekny in the Hoggar mountains. It was occupied until about 6000 BC by people who had begun a simple form of farming – they did not sow seeds, but knew and cared for wild plants. Other people from the upper Niger region may have moved into the Sahara at about the same time.

Painters of the Sahara

The people of the Sahara progressed from animal-hunting to animal-rearing, especially cattle. The appearance of pottery is also evidence of a more settled way of life. Their civilization is shown by the number of drawings and paintings on rock walls and in ravines. This art was continued for 7,000 years, and can be divided into

This village (pictured in colour on pages 32/33), like others in the Nile valley, owes its prosperity to the great river. When the river floods each year, it spreads mud over the land, fertilizing the soil. Irrigation channels have been dug to carry water to dry areas.

The people's crude mud and brick houses are built near to their cultivated plots, which are criss-crossed by a vast network of canals. The farmers prepare the soil with wooden hoes, spades and hand-ploughs. Then they scatter the wheat and millet seeds, letting their sheep and goats trample the soil to dig the seeds in deeper.

They use asses and oxen to help with the work, or for transport. The river is busy with small craft, made of the papyrus reed that grows on the banks alongside date palms. The people use their boats to trade along the river, for fishing and to hunt marsh birds.

This rock painting (left) from Tin Tazarift in the Sahara shows a canoe with animal heads at each end and a pair of hunters. Below it is a drawing showing the landscape of Tassili n'Ajjer, a hilly tableland northwest of the Hoggar mountains in the Sahara. This site is rich in Neolithic rock paintings and engravings.

These oxen were drawn by an artist at Tassili n'Ajjer over 5,000 years ago. The turned-down horns of the animal suggests a domestic beast, not a wild one. A large number of cattle pictures, some of large herds, date from this period. Owning a large herd was probably the mark of a rich person.

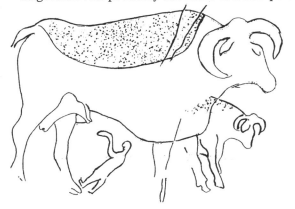

The wild buffalo above has spreading horns. It comes from a rock engraving at Afara Mella, Wadi Djerat in the Tassili n'Ajjer region. The men appear to be hunters.

Papyrus boats like the two shown below were used on the Nile and on other African rivers. The top boat is a simple raft made of reed stalks. The other is boat-shaped. Boats like this are still used on Lake Chad.

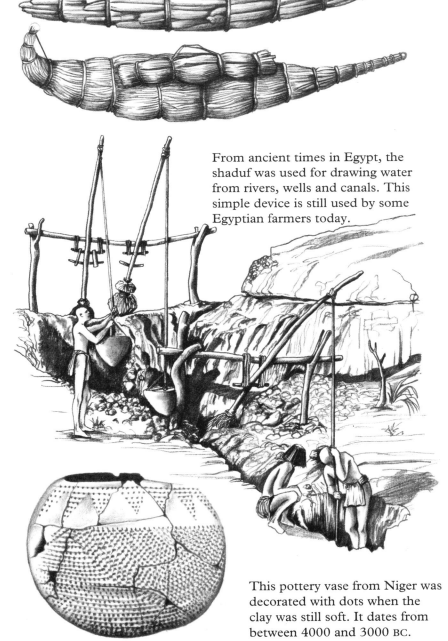

various periods, from the style of the painting. Paintings before about 5000 BC belong to the Hunting Period. Then comes the Pastoral or Cattle Period, to about 1000 BC, followed by the Horse Period, when horses and wheeled carts are shown. Last of all was the Camel Period, from about AD 200.

In all these rock paintings there are many other animals, including wild animals, and plants. There are human figures, too. People are shown farming, hunting and fighting. There are scenes of communal life – people making clothes, body-painting, talking, even making love, as well as drawings of boats and carts.

Civilization in early Egypt

Around 3000 BC the Sahara began to dry out, and its people were forced to move to the flood plain of the River Nile, to ensure a water supply. In the great depression (an area below sea level) of the Fayum (Egypt) water was still plentiful. Here people grew cereals and reared animals, while still hunting and fishing. The great culture of Naqada (so named after the site of important finds) was founded, beginning the rise of Egyptian civilization.

People had earlier begun building small towns and villages in Upper Egypt, the southern lands beside the Nile. They built with mud bricks and made pottery. They baked bread and made beer. They had a hierarchical social structure with a noble class and a leader. Later (3500 to 3300 BC) these people had moved north to Lower Egypt around the Nile delta. As the climate became drier, they were forced to irrigate their fields. Farmers used a new tool, the spade. The leader was becoming a kingly figure, and there were marked differences in burials for different classes of people, with elaborate tombs, decorated inside.

From ancient times in Egypt, the shaduf was used for drawing water from rivers, wells and canals. This simple device is still used by some Egyptian farmers today.

This pottery vase from Niger was decorated with dots when the clay was still soft. It dates from between 4000 and 3000 BC.

9 CENTRAL AND SOUTHERN AFRICA

The map shows some of the major Middle and Late Stone Age sites in central and southern Africa.

A T L A N T I C
O C E A N

Fernando Poo

Lopo

Libreville

Zaire

Moussanda
Bitorri
Kinshasa
Kongo Dia Vanga
Dimba
Ntadi Hradi

Lupemba

Tshito

Museque

Kamoa
Mose
Mulundwa

Bembezi

Broken Hill
Victoria Falls
Gwisho

Zambezi

Inyanga

Limpopo

Magudi

Orange

Modder River
Tugela
Umfolosi
Karridene

Cape Flats
Zitzikama
East London
Oakhurst

Much of central and southern Africa is forested. The equatorial rain forest is home to a range of animals, which inhabit the different layers of the forest. In the treetops, which get most sunlight and rain, there are birds and small monkeys. Lower down there are chimpanzees, parrots, butterflies, snakes and other reptiles. People in the forest were restricted to ground level, living among the roots and undergrowth. They shared their living quarters with okapi, gorillas and forest elephants.

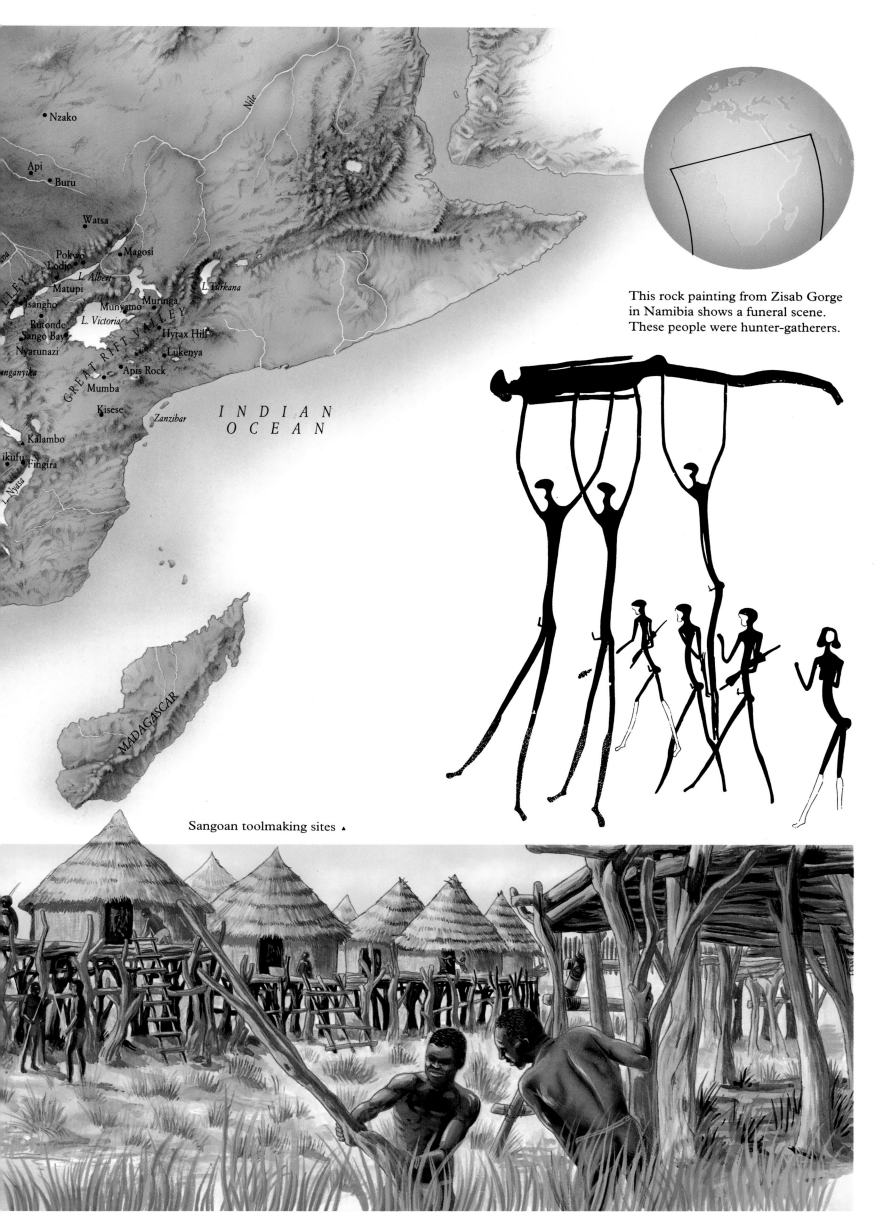

This rock painting from Zisab Gorge in Namibia shows a funeral scene. These people were hunter-gatherers.

Sangoan toolmaking sites ▲

Nzako

Api
Buru

Watsa

Pokwo
Lodjo
Magosi
Matupi
L. Albert
Isangho
Munyamo
Muringa
L. Turkana
Rutonde
L. Victoria
Sango Bay
Hyrax Hill
Nyarunazi
Apis Rock
Lukenya
anganyika
Mumba
Kisese
Zanzibar
Kalambo
ikufu
Fingira
L. Nyasa

Nile

GREAT RIFT VALLEY

LLEY

INDIAN OCEAN

MADAGASCAR

9 CENTRAL AND SOUTHERN AFRICA

An engraving of ostriches and rhinoceroses, from Kisese in Tanzania.

Africa was the continent on which, so far as we know, human beings first appeared. The first human-like beings were dwellers of the grassy plains, although their primitive ancestors had probably been forest-dwellers. A characteristic of human evolution has been people's ability to adapt to new environments – such as cold tundra or hot desert. For humans to return to the tropical forests was another challenge, for the forest environment presented many difficulties.

The Sangoan toolmakers

The Sangoan toolmakers were people named after Sango Bay on the shores of Lake Victoria, where tools made by them were found in 1920. They lived in both East and West Africa, about 50,000 years ago. Later, some of their traditions were carried on by the Lupemban people (named after Lupemba in Zaire).

The Sangoans probably established themselves on wooded river banks, rather than in the forest depths, during a period when a moister climate allowed the equatorial forest to spread. The Lupembans, noted for their well-made stone tools, including lance-shaped blades, were able to penetrate more deeply into the forest. Their culture took over from that of the Sangoans.

The spread of forest-cultures

Little is known of these people's way of life, because the rainforest has destroyed or hidden most traces of their communities. They gathered food from the soil and the undergrowth. Most foods had to be eaten at once before they spoilt in the hot, damp atmosphere. The people cut and shaped wood into simple utensils, and for temporary shelters used branches, bark and lianas (creepers).

These forest toolmaking cultures extended as far north as the River Niger and the fringes of the Sahara. Here they met new conditions, and other cultures, and change resulted. In the east and south, however, on the great plains of Africa, human life went on much as it had for thousands of years before. The plains were rich in animal life, and people lived by hunting.

There were innovations, however, arising from changes in the natural environment, especially near the

This settlement (pictured in colour on pages 36/37) on the shores of Lake Turkana in central-eastern Africa (modern Ethiopia-Kenya) is in an area ideal for hunting and fishing. Around the lake shore are grassy plains abounding in animal life, and the lake itself provides fish and birds.

The villagers use small reed boats to fish from. Reeds are also used to make their houses, which are raised on piles sunk into the marshy ground at the lakeside. This means the houses are safe from flooding, and also gives protection from wild animals such as lions and leopards.

The men hunt and trap antelope and small animals and birds. Fish is an important food, which they catch with bone-tipped spears and with nets. The women gather wild cereals from the grassy plains. Food is plentiful. As a result the people can enjoy a fairly relaxed way of life. Everyone works together to keep the community flourishing.

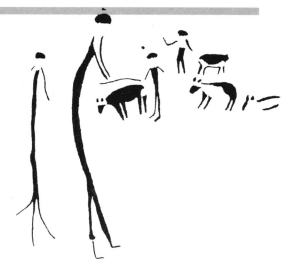

Varieties of cultivated plants grown in prehistoric Africa.
1 Coracan, a cereal grown in Ethiopia.
2 Sorghum, a plant similar to sweetcorn.
3 Chinese vine, a legume (relative of the pea and bean) grown in West Africa.
4 Candle millet, which tolerates a dry climate.
5 Plant and tuber of the yam. The starchy tuber is cooked.

A rock painting of a group of human figures – adults and children – with dogs, from Du Kaw Mtea in Tanzania.

This antelope from Da Kinyasi, Tanzania, is engraved with stripes and shown in a realistic pose, as if it is licking itself.

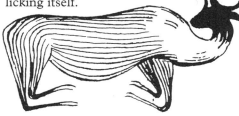

coast (the sea level rose at the end of the Ice Age). Fishing became more important, and to hunt large grassland animals such as buffalo, gnu and the zebra-like quagga, people made better weapons, of which the most important was the bow and arrow.

Caves and rock shelters

Southern Africa offered people some of the richest food resources anywhere in the world. Hunting communities could establish themselves for long periods on one site, and follow other pursuits besides hunting. This is shown by the examples of rock art surviving in Zimbabwe, Tanzania and Namibia.

From about 2,000 years ago, the hunter-gatherers were succeeded over large areas of southern Africa by more advanced farming peoples, who knew the skills of metalworking. These people were perhaps the ancestors of the Bantu-speaking peoples who later moved into southern Africa from the north and west. Before this time, farming in southern Africa was unknown – although some people in the south-west were nomadic herders, who wandered from pasture to pasture with herds of cattle.

ROCK ART
Before people could record or express their thoughts in writing, they created other forms of self-expression. Painting on rock is one form which has been preserved for thousands of years.

The art of primitive people is the only clue we have to their thoughts and ideas about the world. The 20 million rock drawings so far discovered in Europe, Africa, Asia, America and Australia make up an enormous archive, documenting the evolution of human beings for many thousands of years.

Earliest of all are the pictures made by the First Hunters, people who lived before the bow had been invented.

Next comes the art of the Advanced Hunters, for whom the bow was a principal weapon. Wild animals, the hunters' prey, figure largely in the paintings and drawings of these hunters. When the Herders and Animal-Rearers appeared, their pictures often showed the animals they kept, such as sheep and cattle.

The Farming People lived in a more complex and settled society. These people drew human figures and animals, and also gods and goddesses, especially those connected with fertility and the seasons. As civilizations such as that of Ancient Egypt developed, paintings were done on buildings rather than on rocks – on the walls of palaces, temples and tombs. Often paintings had a magical or religious meaning.

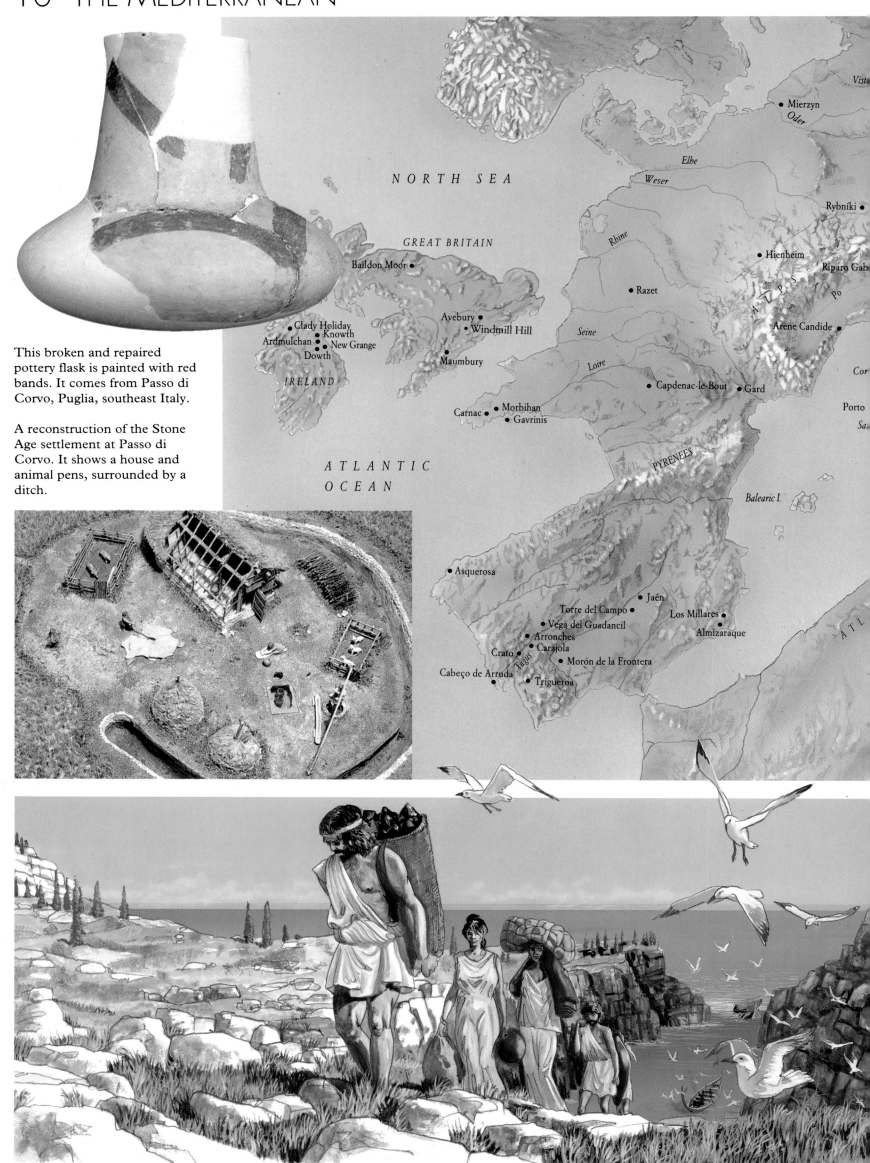

This broken and repaired pottery flask is painted with red bands. It comes from Passo di Corvo, Puglia, southeast Italy.

A reconstruction of the Stone Age settlement at Passo di Corvo. It shows a house and animal pens, surrounded by a ditch.

NORTH SEA

GREAT BRITAIN

Baildon Moor

Clady Holiday
Knowth
Ardmulchan · New Grange
Dowth

IRELAND

Avebury
· Windmill Hill

Maumbury

Carnac · Morbihan
· Gavrinis

ATLANTIC
OCEAN

Mierzyn
Oder

Elbe

Weser

Rhine

Rybníki

Hienheim
Riparo Gab

ALPS
Po

Arene Candide

Seine

Loire

Razet

Capdenac-le-Bout · Gard

Cor

Porto
Sa

PYRENEES

Balearic I.

Asquerosa

Torre del Campo · Jaén
· Vega del Guadancil
Arronches
Crato · Carajola
Cabeço de Arruda · Morón de la Frontera
· Trigueroa

Los Millares ·
Almizaraque

ATL

Vista

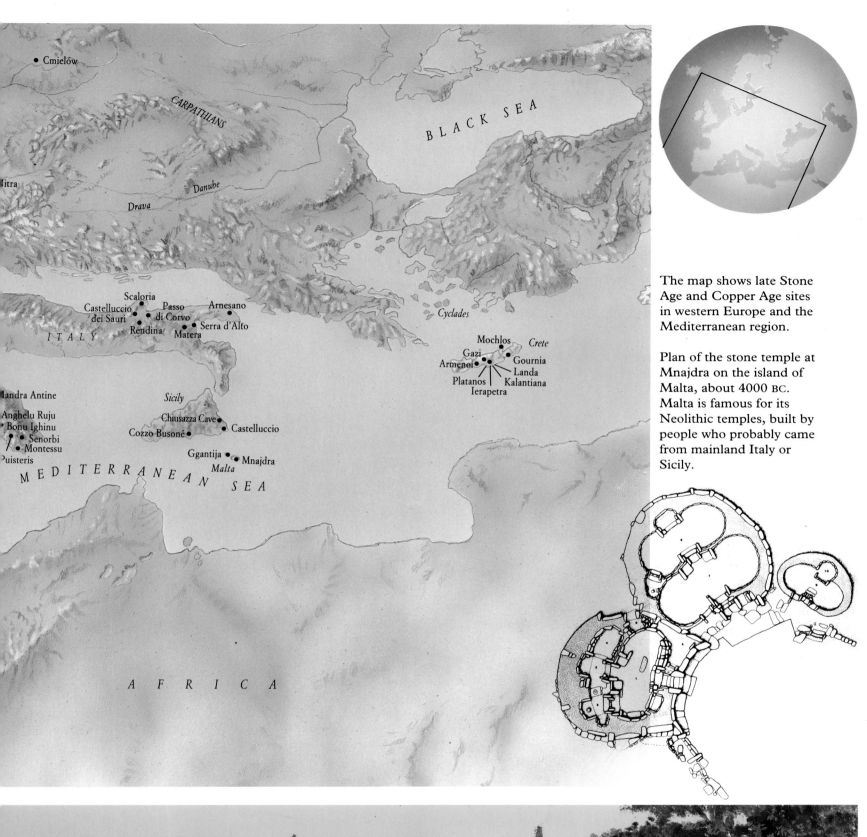

The map shows late Stone Age and Copper Age sites in western Europe and the Mediterranean region.

Plan of the stone temple at Mnajdra on the island of Malta, about 4000 BC. Malta is famous for its Neolithic temples, built by people who probably came from mainland Italy or Sicily.

The new cultures of the late Stone Age and early Metal Age spread throughout Europe, but especially around the Mediterranean. Here people began to cross the ocean to settle new lands, instead of simply moving on foot overland. They had new metal tools (made first from copper and then from bronze), and with these tools they were able to make better boats.

Stone Age sailors

However, even before the new tools appeared, people had ventured out to sea and early seafarers had explored parts of the Mediterranean. Trading in obsidian (volcanic glass, prized for toolmaking) went on across the sea from the main source-areas in the Aeolian Islands, Sardinia and Sicily. Such voyages required courage and determination, as well as navigation skills.

The clearest proof of prehistoric seafaring is that people settled on islands, such as Malta, and took distinct cultures from one area to another, separated by water. This movement of people allowed ideas about technology and religion to be exchanged, as well as trade goods. This is how Stone Age culture spread.

Villages in Italy

In the western and central Mediterranean there was a considerable development of 'colonies', settlements founded by groups of settlers moving into new areas. Farmers had moved into southeast Italy before 5000 BC, and regions in the east, beside the Ionian and Adriatic seas, became thickly populated with village-settlements like the one found at Passo di Corvo, which was built between 4700 and 3650 BC.

These villages were enclosed by one or more ditches. The ditches were possibly for irrigation and drainage. At Passo di Corvo there are one hundred ditches, in the

A figure of a goddess, found at Muhata, Israel. About 5000 BC.

shape of a letter C. The people of these villages were farmers, who made decorated pottery. They grew wheat and barley, and reared sheep and goats. Around the remains of their houses wells, burial sites and traces of their crops have been found.

Along the north Mediterranean, as far west as Spain, people settled either in caves or in small settlements of simple houses. They kept sheep, goats, pigs and oxen, and caught large sea fish such as tuna and swordfish.

In the small bay of Mnajdra (pictured in colour on pages 40/41) on Malta, ships from across the Mediterranean are welcomed by the local people. The settlement is dominated by the stones of one of the island's largest Stone Age temples. The ships carry trade goods, which the people carry up from the rocky bay. Some carry amphoras, large jars with pointed ends.

These early inhabitants of Malta grew cereals, lentils and vetch, and kept sheep, oxen and pigs. They were also fishermen. Above all, the island seems to have been a religious centre, ruled probably by a priesthood who had guardianship over a rich treasure.

Archaeologists have studied the stones of the temples built by the Maltese people, but still do not know a great deal about the people themselves or how they supported such a flourishing civilization on a small and not very fertile island.

Malta was like an oasis in the ocean, a port for ships to visit, and an important stopping-off point on the trade routes that connected the different cultures of the Mediterranean.

The Aegean seafarers explored trade routes, in new and larger designs of ship. As early as 6000 BC ships carried obsidian from the island of Melos to neighbouring settlements. On this oval seal (kind of stamp) made in Crete about 2000 BC is a seagoing vessel with oars and a single large sail. Below it is a Bronze Age pottery ornament from the Cyclades Islands, showing a longship with a tall prow.

A relief showing Mediterranean-type ships, from the temple of Tarxien on Malta.

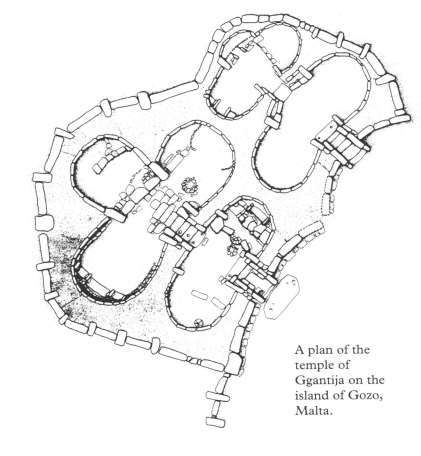

A plan of the temple of Ggantija on the island of Gozo, Malta.

Links between east and west

Copper-using peoples lived along the coasts of southern Spain and Portugal. There are interesting links between these peoples at the western end of the Mediterranean and peoples living in the eastern Mediterranean. At Los Millares in southern Spain, for example, there are remains of a settlement built about 2340 BC. Around it was a thick stone wall with ramparts, unlike any other in western Europe. Its closest similarity is with the fortifications of Chalandriani on the island of Sira, one of the Cyclades islands in the Aegean Sea (between Greece and Turkey).

Items such as pottery, domestic utensils and brooches also link settlements in Spain with settlements in the Cyclades and other islands – suggesting that these Spanish farmers may in fact have come (by ship) from the far end of the Mediterranean.

Malta

People settled on Malta some time before 3500 BC, probably reaching the island by boat from southern Italy and Sicily. On Malta people reared sheep, oxen and pigs, and grew crops of wheat, barley and lentils. They built large stone temples, carved out of the rock, such as those at Mnajdra and Ggantija on the smaller island of Gozo. They buried their dead in small rock tombs. This flourishing culture came to an end before 2500 BC, probably destroyed by metal-using invaders from Italy.

A map of Malta and Gozo, showing the sites of temples.

The map shows settlement sites in Central Europe during the Bronze Age.

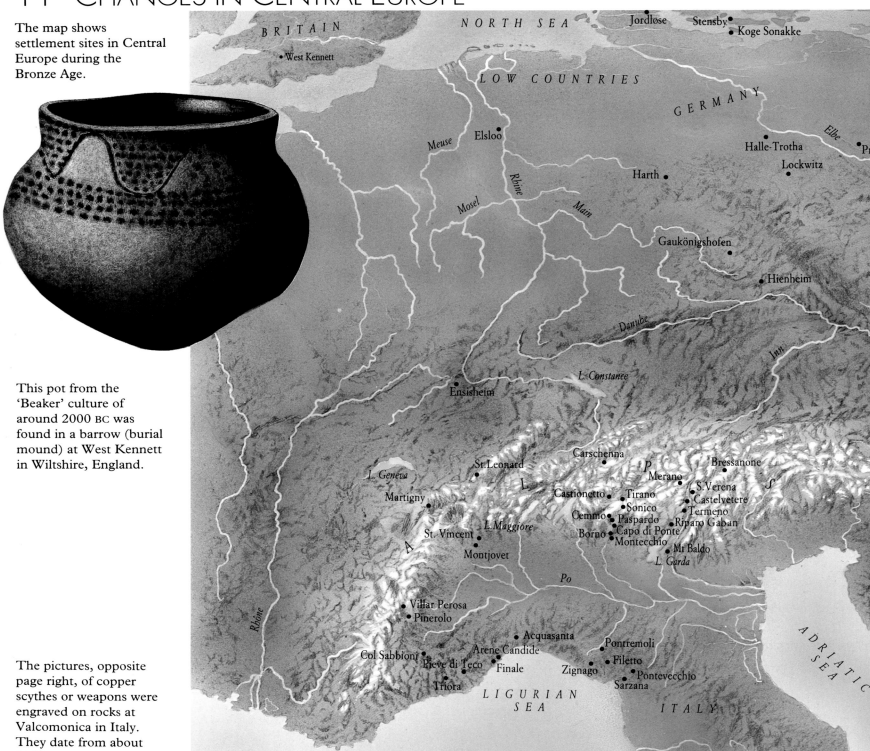

This pot from the 'Beaker' culture of around 2000 BC was found in a barrow (burial mound) at West Kennett in Wiltshire, England.

The pictures, opposite page right, of copper scythes or weapons were engraved on rocks at Valcomonica in Italy. They date from about 2500 to 2000 BC.

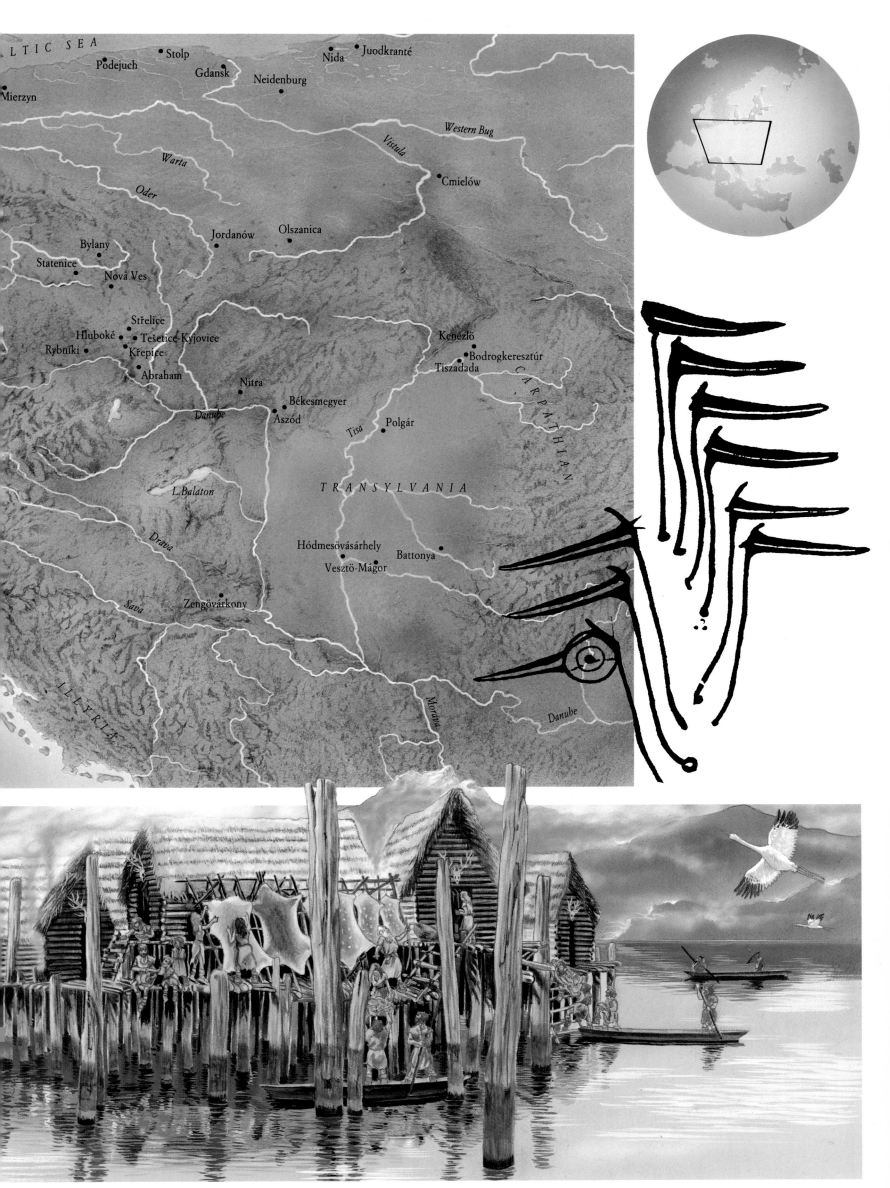

11 CHANGES IN CENTRAL EUROPE

As early as 5000 BC farmers lived across central and eastern Europe, including the Danube and Hungarian plains. These farming peoples moved north and west, taking advantage of the fertile soils of the river valleys and also clearing forests in what are now Slovakia, the Czech Republic, Hungary and Germany.

Village life

The mainstay of life was cereal-growing, with only a small amount of animal-grazing. People lived in villages in houses that were very large – on average 30 metres (98ft) long by 8 metres (26ft) wide, made of a massive wooden framework weatherproofed with mud and clay. Sometimes houses were arranged in an orderly pattern, but more often they were scattered haphazardly.

People seem not to have lived continuously on the same site, though they did reoccupy abandoned sites. They moved on when the soil was no longer fertile enough to give adequate crops. The village of Colonia-Lidenthal in Germany seems to show at least seven periods of occupation – each ten years followed by a gap of fifty years – by a community of about 20 families. A similar story is told by finds at Bylany (Czech Republic), where people seem to have lived in one place for as long as 370 years, and in the Netherlands, where settlements may have lasted still longer.

Many settlements over wide areas show similarities, for example in the kind of pottery that was used, and in the types of houses, wells and drainage ditches. Most houses were big enough for up to 20 people, who were probably related. As many as 400 people might live in one village, like the one found at Sittard in the Netherlands (dating from about 4000 BC).

A typical Beaker vase, undecorated around the middle but with cord-markings around the neck. Such pottery spread widely across Europe. It was often buried in graves.

This copper pendant with a double spiral comes from Stollhof in Austria, around 3000 BC.

Lakeside dwellers

Around 3000 BC farmers travelled along the Mediterranean shores, to colonize southern France and Spain. They moved into the lakelands of northern Italy and the Alpine valleys.

This village (pictured in colour on pages 44/45) is on the shores of a lake in Switzerland. The houses are raised on platforms, supported by wooden piles sunk into the mud.

The wooden huts have pitched roofs of thatch, and have two rooms inside. There is an outer open-sided part, like a porch or shed, used for butchering and skinning animals.

In the nearby forests the hunters kill deer, elk and wild boar. They also shoot lake water birds and migratory birds with their bows. Animal skins are dressed on poles alongside the houses, and antlered skulls are hung over the doorways.

The people use dugout canoes, made by hollowing out tree trunks with stone axes and fire. They move along the shore, clearing patches of forest for farming. They also fish from the boats, catching salmon and sturgeon breeding in the rivers, and netting other fish from the lake itself.

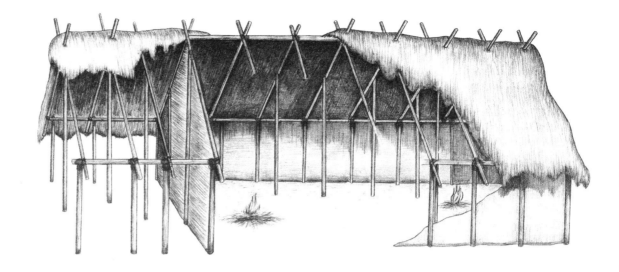

A reconstruction of a Stone Age house at Charavines in the French Alps, a lakeside village built on piles. The house is large, with two hearths for cooking and heating. The people slept on rush mats. The roof extends over an open area, where people can work with some shelter from the wind and rain.

Throughout prehistoric Europe people used scrub and branches to make paths across waterlogged ground. These are the remains of a wooden trackway.

This double-headed stone axe was for ceremonial use. Axes like these are often found with cord-decorated pottery.

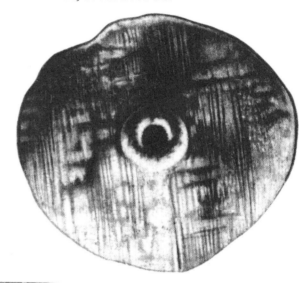

A cartwheel, made from a single slice of tree trunk, from Overyssel in the Netherlands, about 2000 BC.

The first villages built of timber appeared in Switzerland. The houses were built on platforms, raised on wooden piles above the waters of the lake shore. Some houses were big enough for only one family, but others were much larger. There were villages with as many as 75 houses, each roughly 6 by 3 metres (19 by 10ft), with two rooms and often a porch. The population of these lakeshore villages varied from about 120 to as many as 370 people.

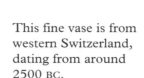

A Beaker drinking cup decorated with stripes, from Brittany in France, dating from around 2600 BC.

Beaker people

During the Copper Age, a common culture was spreading throughout central and western Europe, as far west as the British Isles. This culture can be traced by the use of the easily identifiable 'Beaker' pottery, which was common wherever its makers went.

Many theories have been suggested about where these 'Beaker people' came from originally. What is clear is that they had a great deal of energy. They moved in small groups, with no permanent attachment to the land in one region, and were welcomed by the peoples they encountered because of their technical knowledge.

The Beaker colonists reached the British Isles about 2000 BC. It was in this way that the use of copper probably arrived in Britain.

This fine vase is from western Switzerland, dating from around 2500 BC.

The map shows the spread of the Indo-European languages, from their supposed origins among peoples north of the Black Sea.

Between 4000 and 2000 BC people from the east moved across Europe, bringing with them a new family of languages: Indo-European. Why they moved is not clear, but it probably had to do with overcrowding of homelands where pastures were becoming drier and less fertile. People from the Eurasian plains moved into the forests of Europe, and also south into the Mediterranean and the Middle East.

Eventually, these human migrations followed several main routes. One took them south across the Bosporus into Anatolia (this movement produced the Hittite culture). Others led peoples into India and Iran, into Greece, and into central Europe.

The newcomers absorbed elements of the cultures they met, usually gaining supremacy through their superior weapons and military skills. Wherever they established themselves, their languages gradually changed, to produce the various branches of the Indo-European language family we know today (see page 51). From this cultural migration sprang the shoots of the later Greek, Celtic and Roman civilizations.

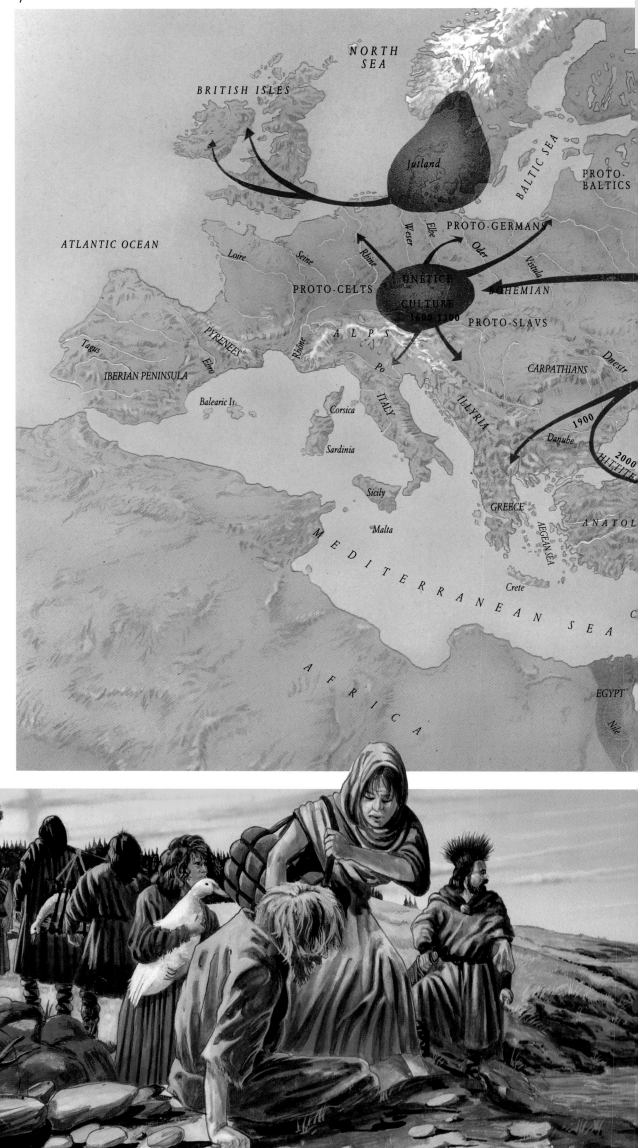

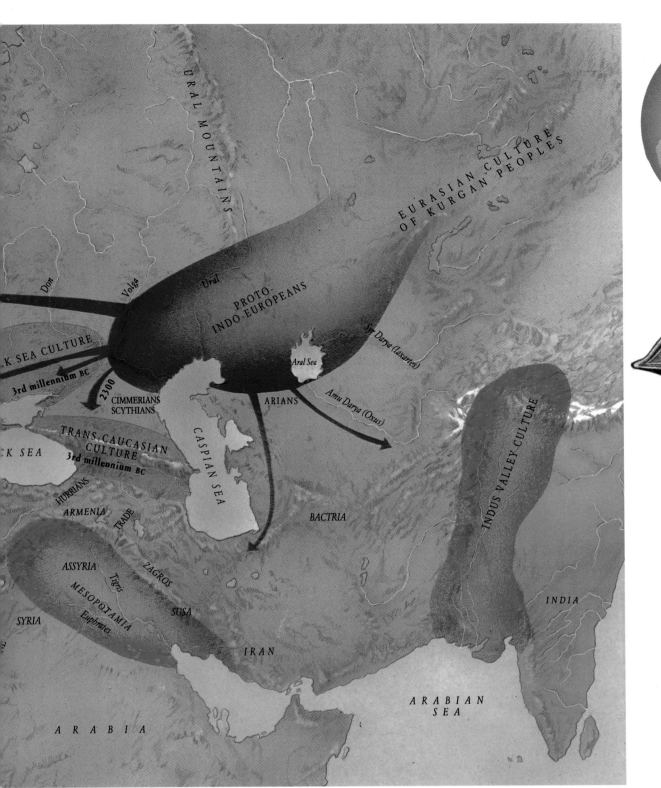

EURASIAN CULTURE
OF KURGAN PEOPLES

URAL MOUNTAINS

Don
Volga
Ural
Sir Darya (Jaxartes)

PROTO-
INDO-EUROPEANS

Aral Sea

...CK SEA CULTURE

3rd millennium BC

2300
CIMMERIANS
SCYTHIANS

ARIANS

Amu Darya (Oxus)

TRANS-CAUCASIAN
CULTURE
3rd millennium BC

...CK SEA

CASPIAN SEA

INDUS VALLEY CULTURE

HURRIANS

ARMENIA

TRADE

BACTRIA

ASSYRIA

ZAGROS

Tigris

MESOPOTAMIA

SUSA

INDIA

Euphrates

SYRIA

IRAN

ARABIA

ARABIAN
SEA

A bronze war axe, from around 2000 BC, found in Hungary. The decoration is very elaborate, and typical of the Indo-European peoples who made such weapons.

12 New Peoples, New Languages

Experts have many theories about the origins of the great movements of people and cultures. Groups of people who already had some things in common, such as their pottery and toolmaking methods, were now influenced by languages derived from a common source – the so-called Indo-European parent-language. We know that numerous modern languages are descended from this parent language but to establish where the 'original speakers' came from is difficult.

Horse-tamers of the steppes
The story begins with the horse. Some time before 2000 BC groups of farmers and herders, with strong leaders and social bonds, and speaking similar languages, settled on the grassy plains north of the Black Sea and the Caspian Sea. Once hunters, they had domesticated the wild horse and become animal breeders.

These horse-tamers spread out in all directions, travelling far because they had horses and wheeled vehicles. With these advantages, they found it easier to subdue and rule rivals rather than merely plunder their homes. The peoples of the steppes rode their horses and drove their herds westwards in search of better pastures.

The Kurgan culture
'Kurgan' is a Russian word meaning hill. The steppes people who bear the name Kurgan buried their dead in single graves beneath hill-like mounds. Around 2400-2300 BC they moved into the lands of the Caucasus and around the Black Sea, whose inhabitants had benefited from contact with the civilizations of the Euphrates

The great migrations were made possible by the invention of the wheel. Wheels were used by the farmers of Mesopotamia around 3000 BC and the use of wheeled carts spread rapidly across the plains of Eurasia. However, people who lived in mountains or in regions with bumpy terrain preferred the wooden sled or a beast of burden such as the ass or camel.

The first carts (seen from the rear and the side below) had four wheels and were made to move heavy loads. Their wheels were made from solid pieces of wood, cut from tree trunks. With the invention of the spoked wheel, the lightweight war chariot came into being.

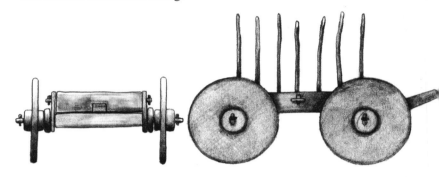

region. The newcomers absorbed these benefits, and from this grew a richer civilization. Its symbol is the battle-axe, made by its warlike people. They were the Hittites, the first people whose language we know to be Indo-European.

Single-grave burials and battle-axes begin to appear elsewhere – in the Balkans about 2000 BC, then as far north as Denmark, Sweden, Norway and the British Isles.

The Únětice and Urnfield cultures
In Bohemia and southern Germany the Indo-European-speaking newcomers founded one of the richest prehistoric cultures. It is called Únětice, from a site near Prague (Czech Republic). This is the earliest Bronze Age culture in central Europe. From here, they made

This scene (pictured in colour on pages 48/49) shows a travelling group of Indo-European speakers struggling to cross a river in central Europe. These peoples had been on the move for generations, moving with their animals and carts, and protected by warriors armed with copper weapons.

On these long journeys the people carried their possessions in wheeled carts, pulled by horses. They traded with people they met, and often mingled with the local population, giving rise to new cultures.

Even the small horse of the steppes changed from its wild form. Cross-bred with the larger horses of Europe, it gave rise to a larger, faster breed which could be ridden. Horse-riding warriors – cavalry – became a powerful new weapon for wars of conquest.

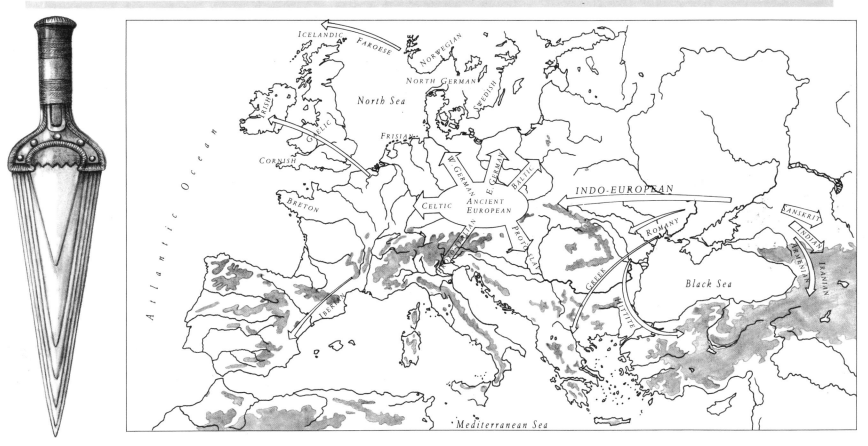

contact with the Beaker culture of western Europe.

Around 1300 BC the people of the Únětice culture began to cremate their dead and bury the ashes in urns in cemeteries. From this comes a new name: Urnfield culture.

New skills in mining and metalworking, in bronze, made these people more adept at making trade goods and weapons, and they probably also began to use the plough. Their culture, through migration and trade, influenced much of Europe. Around this time, Indo-European-speaking peoples also migrated south to Italy, the Balkans and Greece. Around 2000 BC an important group can be traced in the Indus and Ganges river valleys of the Indian sub-continent.

Far left: Bronze dagger made by people of the Únětice culture. From Germany.

The map (above) shows migrations of peoples and the development of new language groups.

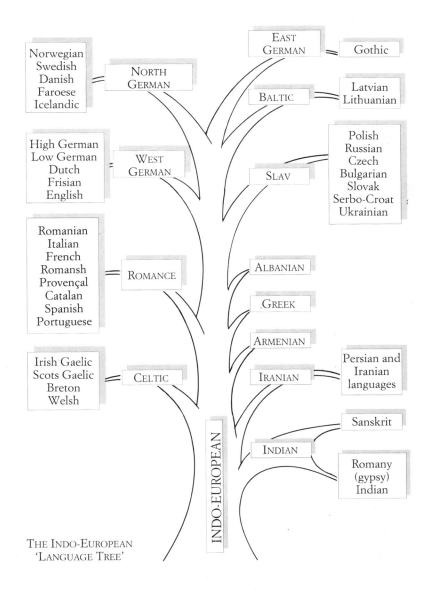

THE INDO-EUROPEAN 'LANGUAGE TREE'

The Indo-European language family includes most of the languages spoken by modern Europeans, as well as a number of languages spoken in south and west Asia. These languages had a "parent language" which was spoken before 4000 BC by people living in east-central Europe. By migrating, they spread their language to new areas. The suggestion that different languages of Europe and Asia had a common ancestor was first made in the early 1700s. It is now possible to draw up a "family tree", like that on the right, showing how the various branches of the Indo-European language family are related. There are many other language families.

13 MOTHER GODDESSES AND TOMBS

The map shows some megalithic (stone monument) sites in western and southern Europe.

A Mother Goddess figure, on a throne with two cats at her side. She is in the act of giving birth. This statuette, less than 12cm (5in) high, comes from Çatal Hüyük and was made around 6000 BC.

THE MOTHER GODDESS

A 'mother goddess' appears as a symbol on ornaments and painted pottery throughout Europe and the Middle East during the Stone Age. Most of these images date from between 6500 to 3500 BC, but there are also earlier examples, and the Mother Goddess continues to appear in art throughout the Bronze Age.

The giver of life was represented in childbirth. There was also a bird-woman (the giver of nourishment) and a death-symbol (a dried bone). Life, death and the renewal of living things were central to the early human experience. In art this theme was manifested by lines which are always in motion – circling and twisting, spiralling and zigzagging, coiling like snakes. These moving lines are symbols of the energy of nature, and of the life-death cycle.

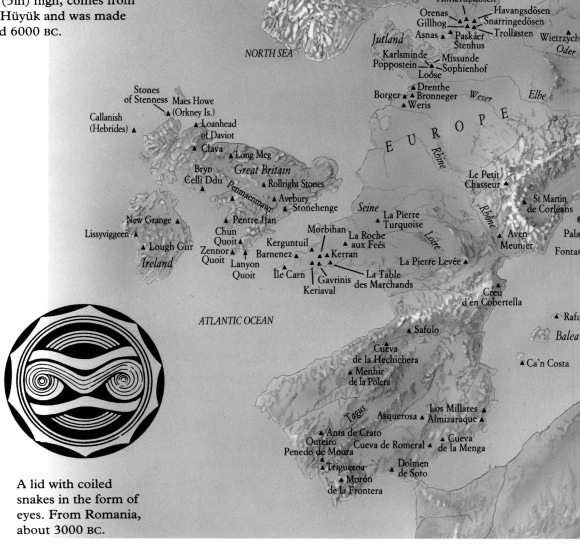

A lid with coiled snakes in the form of eyes. From Romania, about 3000 BC.

This terracotta statue of a Mother Goddess, lying with her head on a pillow, was found in a temple on Malta. Below it is a dolmen, a table-shaped stone monument, for a burial. This is the dolmen of Lanyon Quoit in Cornwall, England.

13 MOTHER GODDESSES AND TOMBS

1

2

A megalith (from two Greek words meaning 'large stone') is a huge stone. Such stones were set up by people in the late Stone Age and early Bronze Age as monuments. Some are rings of stones, others solitary upright stones.

The Mother Goddess

People also made stone figures of the deities they worshipped. A principal deity was the Mother Goddess. She represents nature, the force that touched every aspect of life in prehistoric times, controlling the natural cycles of reproduction. Female figures with huge breasts and bellies symbolized the life-renewing force of nature.

The cult of the Mother Goddess flourished around the Mediterranean Sea and the Middle East. It may have reflected a belief about religion and social order, in which women played the central role and mothers were more important than fathers. Male deities were usually unimportant figures.

This seems to have changed with the arrival of the nomadic ancestors of the Indo-European speakers. Their society was headed by a warrior-leader (a man).

The Mother Goddess assumed various forms. In one she was the goddess of agriculture, and giver of the fruits of harvest, especially wheat. She was portrayed realistically as a naked woman with her hands resting on a swollen (pregnant) belly. She was also linked with the seasons in the form of a snake-goddess, and with death

Examples of megaliths in Europe

1 Trollasten, Stora Kopingem, Sweden.
2 Callanish, Isle of Lewis, Scotland.
3 Stenness, Orkney Islands, Scotland.
4 Poilnaborne, Co. Clare, Ireland.
5 Pentre Ifan, Wales.
6 Menhir de la Polera, Burgos, Spain.
7 Men an Tol, Morvah, Cornwall.
8 Trethevy Quoit, Cornwall.
9 Lagatjart, Brittany, France.
10 Anta de Candieira, Portugal.
11 Anta de St Genns, Portugal.
12 Anta de Cuotade de Barbacena, Portugal.
13 Montefrio, Andalusia, Spain.
14 Dolmen, Valencia Das Juan, Spain.

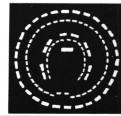

A human head, in stylized form, from Ireland, between 3500-3200 BC. It is carved in flint, with gaping mouth and coiling snakes around the eyes.

in the form of a bird of prey or as a whitened bone. In whatever form she was represented, the Mother Goddess was the same, mother of life but also mother of death and of renewal.

Stonehenge (pictured in colour on pages 52/53) is probably the best-known megalithic monument in Europe. It is about 13 kilometres (8 miles) north of Salisbury in Wiltshire, England.

What we see today are the remains of several stone circles, put up at different times. The work was immense, requiring the collective effort of people from many communities, and the movement of enormous stones over considerable distances.

The people who built Stonehenge had to dig large holes into which they upturned the stones, with the help of levers and ropes. Towers of tree trunks were probably used to help the people raise the huge stones. At least 200 men would have been needed to raise each stone upright – the stones weigh as much as 50 tonnes (50 tons) each. Lintels were laid across the tops of the standing stones.

The original Stonehenge was built around 3000 BC, but it was enlarged and altered during the next 1,500 years. The stonework is so skilful that some people have suggested that architects from Mycenae helped construct it. There is also a theory that the stones were positioned to observe the movements of the sun and moon during the year.

Plan of Stonehenge

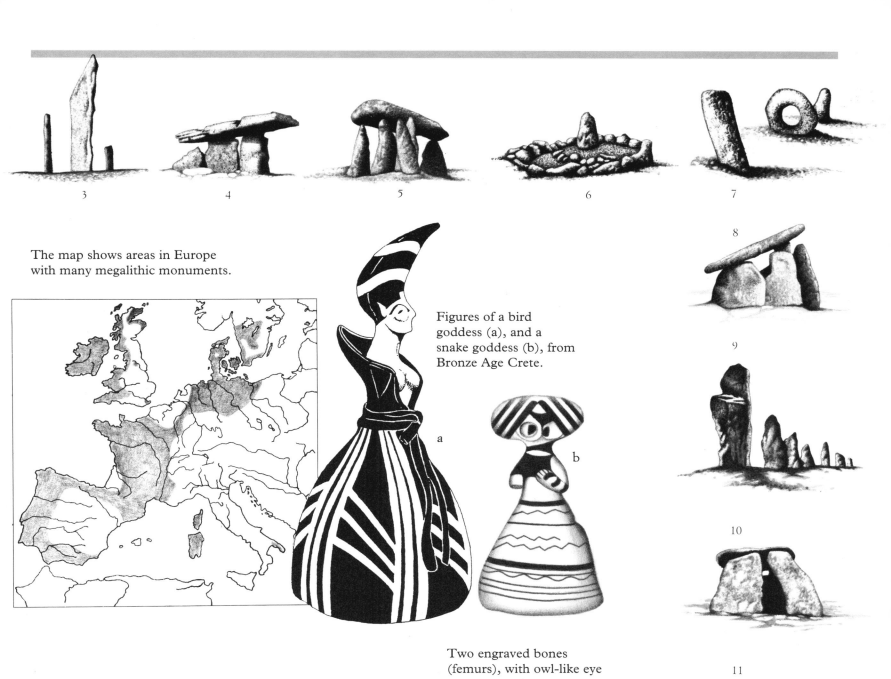

The map shows areas in Europe with many megalithic monuments.

Figures of a bird goddess (a), and a snake goddess (b), from Bronze Age Crete.

Two engraved bones (femurs), with owl-like eye decoration. One c) comes from northeast France (about 5000 BC); the other d) from Almeria in Spain, about 2500 BC. The bone is a death-symbol, while the owls' eyes are a divine sign of rebirth – another aspect of the Mother Goddess.

Egg-shaped tombs

Tombs were egg-shaped. Inside them the dead person was arranged in the curled-up position of an unborn baby. In some burial places, the stones were arranged like the Goddess herself, to represent her breasts, belly, buttocks or even her whole body – there are examples of this in Malta.

The Indo-European speakers brought the idea of single burials to Europe. Before their arrival, people were buried in communal graves or in underground tombs. This reflected the strong ties of village life, in which all the inhabitants were bound by family and community ties.

The great stone monuments are the first examples in western and northern Europe of people working together, and are the oldest forms of permanent architecture known in this part of the world. There are similar megaliths in the Caucasus and Jordan, Ethiopia, India and Japan. However, this does not mean that people in these different places shared the same religious beliefs.

Dolmens (table-shaped arrangements of stones) varied in shape, but all had the same function – as burial places. They were sacred places where people held rites and sacred ceremonies.

KEY: SPREAD OF AGRICULTURE · COPPER AGE · BRONZE · IRON

Upper section (10 000 – 0)

BRITISH ISLES
4800 Neolithic
4100 Long barrows
3900 Corridor tombs
3600 Four-sided tombs
4th mil. Clearing of forest by burning
3000 Migration from mainland Europe of Neolithic hunters using smooth stone axes and crude pottery
3rd mil. Appearance of the wheel
2500-2000 Regular trade across the Channel. Migration of farmers and Neolithic animal rearers
About 2500 Building of Stonehenge
2000-1500 Influences from Spain, France and Germany. Also from the Baltic and the Balkans by way of the Danube and Rhine. Cremation, round barrows. Bronze Age
1500-600 Invasion of northern Britain by the Picts
1472 (legendary date) Invasion of Ireland by the Danae coming from Greece to escape Syrian invasion, across Denmark, which is how it got its name, according to the legend

WESTERN EUROPE
6200-5300 Old Neolithic. Development of cardial pottery culture
5300-4000 Culture of 'Epicardial' pottery
4600-4100 Middle Neolithic
4100-3200 Chassey culture
4th mil. Spread of megaliths
About 3200 Late Neolithic
About 2500 Start of Beaker culture

IBERIAN PENINSULA
6200-5300 Old Neolithic. Development of cardial pottery culture
5300-4000 Culture of 'Epicardial' pottery
4000 Almerian culture
4th mil. Spread of megaliths
3200 Los Millares
3rd mil. Appearance of the wheel
End of 3rd mil. Start of the Bronze Age. Large villages with tradition of metal-working in Portugal

SCANDINAVIA
5900 Maglemosean and Kunda cultures: wood-working
4500 Narva culture (Baltic)
4200 Ertebolle (shellfish gatherers), Denmark
4th-3rd mil. Farming appeared in Sweden
3800 Funnel beaker culture
3100 Amphora culture
After 3000 Culture of corded ware pottery
3rd mil. Appearance of the wheel. Start of the Bronze Age. Spread of megaliths

CENTRAL EUROPE
5800 Spread of of farming
5500 Linear pottery
5th mil. Spread of wool and flax production
4700 Decorated pottery
4500 Linear decoration
4100 Rössin, site in north Germany
4th mil. Use of plough
4th-3rd mil. Colonization of the Alps
3900 Michelsberg
3300 Amphora culture
3000 Corded ware pottery
3rd mil. Appearance of the wheel
End of 3rd mil. Start of Bronze Age, first of all in Bohemia (Czech.). Spread of megaliths

BOHEMIA AND LOWER GERMANY
1600-1300 Development of Únětice culture after Indo-European migrations. Form of 'Old European' language from which later German, Italian, Baltic, Slav and southern Balkan languages developed

WESTERN BALKANS
6400 Illyria: cardial pottery
6th mil. Start of Chalcolithic (Copper Age)
5500-4300 Culture of Starcevo
5300-4400 Danilo culture
4400-3500 Hvar culture
3rd mil. Appearance of the wheel
End of 3rd mil. Start of Bronze Age

CENTRAL BALKANS
6200-5200 Starcevo-Körös culture
6th mil. Start of Chalcolithic
5200-4300 Vinca culture
4600 Petresto culture in Transylvania
4300-4000 Kurgan migrations
4000-3500 Cernavada culture
3rd mil. Appearance of the wheel
End of 3rd mil. Start of Bronze Age. Appearance of domesticated horse
About 1900 Indo-Europeans move up the Danube into Central Europe

EASTERN BALKANS
7th-4th mil. Spread of more advanced religions and matriarchy
6200-4300 Karanovo culture
6th mil. Start of Chalcolithic
5800-5200 Dnestr-Bug culture in Moldavia and western Ukraine
5200-5000 Linear pottery
5000-3500 Cucuteni culture
4300-4000 Kurgan migrations from east
3rd mil. Appearance of wheel
End of 3rd mil. Start of Bronze Age. Appearance of domesticated horse

Lower section (500 – 10 000)

CENTRAL SOUTHERN AFRICA
100,000 Start of Mesolithic
50,000 Sangoan culture. Beginning of the forest settlement
After 50,000 People in southern Africa abandoned big game hunting. More intensive exploitation of resources. Organized food-gathering on the savannah. Stone tools
35,000-12,000 Lupemban culture, occupation of forest
10,000-5000 Capsian culture of Kenya
6000-4000 Cultivation of millet in Ethiopia and Uganda
5000 First production of pottery in Kenya
3rd mil. Rock art
End 2nd mil. Iron Age in Africa
1st mil. Saharan cities abandoned to desert
End of 1st mil. Great expansion of Bantu iron-workers and animal-herders

NORTH AFRICA
11,000-9000 Highest level of water in Lake Chad, before drying-up begins
8000 Capsian culture. Start of Neolithic. Possibly the first definite forms of animal rearing and then farming
6700 The proto-Neolithic site of Amekni in Hoggar (same date as Jericho), proving that the Sahara was one of the earliest farming regions
From 7th mil. The great age of North African rock art
5000 Sahara starts to dry up and wildlife migrates
1500-1000 Domestication of the horse. First drawings of figures driving chariots

EGYPT
5000-3000 Start of efforts to control the Nile flood waters. Civilization of Egypt made possible by farmers' mastery of irrigation
3800 Start of hieroglyphics
3300 Spread of copper throughout the Nile valley
About 2800 Unification of the old kingdoms of Upper and Lower Egypt under the first pharaohs, ending the prehistoric period

PALESTINE–SYRIA
9000 Pre-Neolithic Natufian culture
8000-6000 Jericho, walled town built by farmers
6000 Old Neolithic
After 5500 Middle Neolithic
After 4000 Ghassul (near Jericho); mud-brick buildings and wall-paintings
After 3500 Foundation of coastal cities. Mesopotamian influences and wide trading
3000 Trade with Egypt. Start of Bronze Age
2500 Foundation of rich cities such as Mari (Sumeria) and Ebla (Syria). Invasion by Hittites and Amorites

MESOPOTAMIA
After 7000 Oldest evidence of cultivated cereals
6000 Rural settlements, simple pottery
After 5000 Qalat-Jarmo Hassuna civilization of Halaf
4000 Start of Chalcolithic. Spread of villages on the seasonally flooded plains. Cities with temples: Obeid, Eridu, Uruk, Kish, Ur
3500 Obeid civilization
3500-3000 Potter's wheel. Painted pottery. Metal scythes
3000 First evidence of writing. Start of Bronze Age
2600 Proto-Dynastic period. Sumerian city state with Ur as capital
2500 Lagash dynasties
2400 Akkad dynasty

IRAN
9000-7000 First farmers, simple pottery
4000 Copper-working. Beginnings of town life at Sialk, Susa and elsewhere
2600 Tombs, carts, multi-coloured pottery. Start of Bronze Age
2300 Elam trades with Mesopotamia
About 2000? Indo-Europeans arrive
900 Medes and Persians

CENTRAL ASIA
4th-3rd mil. Animal rearing and first attempts at farming
2nd mil. Development of agriculture
From 1000 Abandonment of farming and permanent way of life, change to horse-riding nomadic shepherds, spreading across the steppes

RUSSIA–UKRAINE

5th mil. Start of [Copp]er Age. Corded ware [pottery]

3500 End of [Neo]lithic and start of [Bronze] Age in Black Sea [area]. Corded ware [pottery]

[?]mil. Domestication of [horse] and appearance of [rab]bit

[P]ont and Aral [?]ations

[About] 2000 Migrations of [Indo]-Europeans

ITALY–SICILY

SOUTHERN ITALY

6500 Cardial pottery
6000 Rendina, Puglia
5700 Stentinello, Sicily
5200 Passo di Corvo, Scaloria
5000 Serra d'Alto
4400 Diana
3600 Start of Chalcolithic

NORTHERN ITALY

4900 Fiorano
4400 Square-necked pottery culture
3700 Lagozza
3100 Remedello

WESTERN MEDITERRANEAN

SARDINIA AND CORSICA

6200 Old Neolithic, development of cardial pottery
5300 Filiestru
4500 Bonu Ighinu
4000 Ozieri
3600 Basi
3500 Porto Ferro
3000 Start of pre-Nuraghe culture

CENTRAL WESTERN MEDITERRANEAN

5th mil. Spread of Neolithic

MALTA

From 5th mil. Traces of Neolithic society based on animal rearing and farming. Monochrome pottery. Skorba culture. Trade in obsidian and flint from Lipari, Sicily and Pantelleria. Traces of influence of Calabrian-Sicilian culture of Stentinello. Cave tombs

GREECE

6500 First farmers, trade in obsidian
5000 Pottery, especially in Thessaly (Sesklo) and Macedonia
5600 Dimini (fortified site)
3000 Start of Bronze Age
3rd mil. People of Anatolian origin. Indo-European speakers
1600 Mycenaean civilization lasting until about 1100

CRETE

About 6000 First farmer-settlers
About 2000 Towns with palaces, such as Knossos

EGYPT

From 6000 In the Mesolithic cultivation of cereals; rearing of cattle, goats and oxen, pottery making. Colonization of Crete and other islands. Use of the sling. Irrigation of Nile valley and delta by farmers. Various invasions of the Proto Indo-Europeans coming from north of the Black Sea in the 3rd mil.

About 3200 Unification of kingdoms of Upper and Lower Egypt. First Dynasties

ANATOLIA–CYPRUS

9000 Mesolithic Gelbasi and Beldibi
9000-8000 Trade in obsidian to Syria and Palestine
About 7200-6600 Neolithic (pre-pottery)
About 7000 Hacilar, oldest finds of cultivated cereals
6600 Beldiba pottery
6500 Çatal Hüyük. Neolithic
2700 Alalakh palace (Syria)
2600-2500 Start of Bronze Age
2400 Troy II. Gold and silver
2000 Troy III, IV, V. Invasion by the Indo-Europeans (Hittites). Palestine/Assyrian trade with the Indo-Europeans. They reach the Near East: domesticated horse, bit, war chariot, spoked wheel

CYPRUS

About 6000-5200 Neolithic (pre-pottery)
5200 Khirokitia culture, round stone houses

(Top date scale, BC, read top to bottom): 10 000 · 9500 · 9000 · 8500 · 8000 · 7500 · 7000 · 6500 · 6000 · 5500 · 5000 · 4500 · 4000 · 3500 · 3000 · 2500 · 2000 · 1500 · 1000 · 500 · 0

(Bottom date scale, read top to bottom): 500 · 1000 · 1500 · 2000 · 2500 · 3000 · 3500 · 4000 · 4500 · 5000 · 5500 · 6000 · 6500 · 7000 · 7500 · 8000 · 8500 · 9000 · 9500 · 10 000

INDIA

3000 Traces of [farm]ing, animal rearing and [farm]ing in Pakistan and [Afgh]anistan

3000 Farming and [rearin]g of goats, pigs, oxen. [Paint]ed pottery and copper [?]. Civilizations of [?], Amri-Nal, Kulli, [?]. Start of Bronze Age [?] Small town [?]ation in Indus Valley: [Moh]enjo Daro, Harappa I [and] Harappa II

SOUTHEAST ASIA

6th mil. Start of Melanesian migration, probably from China. Neolithic culture of Hoa Bihn in Indo-China. Corded ware pottery
About 4000 Start of Metal Age
About 3000 New migrations from China. Start of rice cultivation
3rd mil. Start of Iron Age. Megaliths in Indonesia
2000-1500 Start of monument (tomb) civilization
About 1000 Dong Son civilization
1st mil. Contacts with Indonesia and Pacific islands

CHINA

About 6000 Start of Neolithic in Yellow River (Huang-He) valley. Domestication of dog, pig, cat and buffalo
Early 4th mil. Start of rice growing
Early 3rd mil. Domestication of horse and sheep. Potter's wheel, fine pottery
2500 Neolithic civilizations with painted pottery at Yangshao-Banpo
2400 Striped pottery at Kanso (up to about 1600). Start of dynastic period
1500 Start of Bronze Age

JAPAN

18,000-12,000 Isolation of Japanese islands from Asian continent
About 1300 Start of Mesolithic Age. Trade in obsidian
About 7000 Start of early Jomon culture
About 5000 Jomon. Start of Neolithic
1500 Mid-Jomon. First farming attempts, ornate pottery, harpoons
1000 End Jomon. Rice cultivation
About 500 Start of Yayoi civilization. Development of farming. Potter's wheel
About 300 Start of Metal Age

NORTH AMERICA

30,000 People move into America from Asia during the Ice Age
10,000-9000 Clovis hunter-gatherer culture, occupying the whole of the North American continent. Great Lakes begin to dry out in the Pleistocene. The plains bison became the sacred animal of archaic hunters
4000 The Eastern peoples developed cold-hammered copper working
3500 Paleo-arctic culture of Alaska. Settlement of Labrador and Greenland
3rd-2nd mil. Start of Neolithic. Wood-working on the North West coast
About 2000 Start of farming in Arizona. Domesticated dogs and turkeys
1st mil. Spread of pottery and farming

CENTRAL AND SOUTHERN AMERICA

9000 Extinction of various species of large animals
8000 Attempts at cultivation in Mexico and the Andes
7000 Seasonally moving herders and farmers of the Andes
5th mil. Start of farming in Mexico, Central America and Andes. Culture of Huaca Prieta in the Andes
From 2500 Start of Olmec culture in Mexico. Cultivation of manioc. Farming in Venezuela, Colombia and Ecuador
2nd mil. Dawn of Maya civilization, Zapotec and Mixtec civilization in Central America
1st mil. Spread of pottery. Chavín culture in Peru

OCEANIA

AUSTRALIA

50,000-35,000 People settle coasts
30,000 Populating of New Guinea
15,000 Spread of hunter-gatherers across Australia. Stone tools, rock paintings
9000 Melanesia settlements
7th mil. Philippines, Celebes, New Guinea, Melanesia, development of cultivation
Early 4th mil. Smooth pottery
End 4th mil. Decorated pottery, 'urn' burials
2nd mil. Main Polynesian conquest. Polynesians voyage to:
1500 Fiji, Samoa
AD **300** Marquesas, Society Is.
AD **400** Easter Island
AD **800** Hawaii
AD **900** New Zealand

15 THE METAL REVOLUTION

The map opposite shows trade routes and sources of raw materials in Europe and the Mediterranean region.

The discovery of metals, and how to extract and use them, was a major change in humankind's exploitation of natural resources. Metalworking called for a completely new technology, quite different from the methods developed to make stone tools. The chart on pages 56/57 shows how agriculture and metalworking developed in different areas.

Copper-working was first practised in Anatolia and Egypt, and before 2000 BC there were metalworking centres in Europe, too. One was in Transylvania (Romania) and the other in the Iberian Peninsula (Spain and Portugal). In central Europe people began to use massive copper axes.

From copper to bronze

To make the advance from copper (which was soft) to a harder metal, bronze, humans had to learn how to add tin to copper in the right amount (10 per cent) to make an alloy, or mixture of two metals – bronze. This discovery was made about 3000 BC.

The new metal-using communities depended on a supply of raw material (ores) and processes to extract them, and turn them into metal that could be made into tools and weapons. They had to trade with unfamiliar peoples, visit distant lands, absorb new customs and ideas. All this was very new to humankind, which before had changed only very slowly over many thousands of years.

Trade and warfare

The demand for metals, first for copper alone, and then also for tin, became part of a new trading economy which spread as far as Poland and Denmark, where people were still using stone tools and had only just begun farming.

The Indo-European-speaking peoples knew about metals. Their society was based on armed warriors serving a chosen god-king, who was advised by a council of elders. Farming peoples who used metal tools, harvested and milled cereals, hunted and tamed horses, and kept herds of cattle, sheep and pigs were living in southern Russia from 2500 BC. Copper, silver and gold objects have been found in their graves.

Changes in society

The arrival in central Europe of these new peoples brought many changes. But metalworking itself was already established, having been brought from Spain and Portugal by the so-called Beaker people. The new technology had obvious benefits for war-making, and all over Europe a new warrior-class began to play a leading part in society.

The Bronze Age

The period between the Stone-Copper Age and the Iron Age is known as the Bronze Age because bronze was the most important metal used to make weapons and tools. Bronze tools were highly prized, because the materials needed to make bronze (copper and tin) were not found everywhere. People had to seek out new sources of the metals. Cyprus was so rich in copper that the Romans gave its name to the metal.

Bronze-using cultures arose in Mesopotamia, Egypt and the Indus valley. Later, bronze-working began in China. The metal revolution was part of humankind's next development – to large, organized civilizations.

A silver jug from a tomb at Maikop in the northern Caucasus Mountains, from around 2000 BC. The decoration of plants and animals includes a wild horse of the Eurasian plains. Wild horses, once hunted for food, became rare. Tamed steppes horses were used for pulling carts. By 1000 BC war horses were beginning to be used.

THE USE OF ENERGY

From about 40,000 years ago, when humans mastered fire, they began to exploit natural energy sources. This was to have a dramatic effect on the world.

Stone Age peoples consumed energy by hunting animals and by gathering plants, and had relatively limited impact on the environment. However, hunting may have helped to drive some species of animals to extinction.

The first farmers began to change the environment more obviously, by clearing forest. They used draught animals (such as oxen and asses), increasing the power at their command, and they increased food production, which led to population growth and trade.

By digging drainage and irrigation ditches, people were able to 'green' arid land, and make it habitable. But by clearing forest indiscriminately, they also began to impoverish the soil in some regions.

Humans began to use heat-technology, to transform clay into pottery, and to smelt metals. They also made use of wind-power, to fill the sails of their ships.

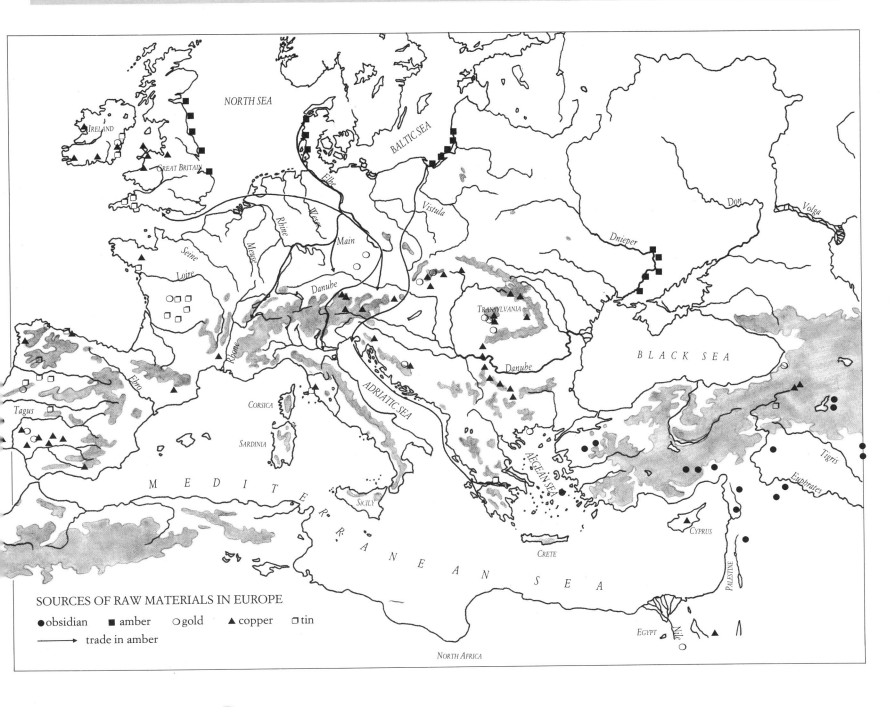

SOURCES OF RAW MATERIALS IN EUROPE

● obsidian ■ amber ○ gold ▲ copper □ tin

——→ trade in amber

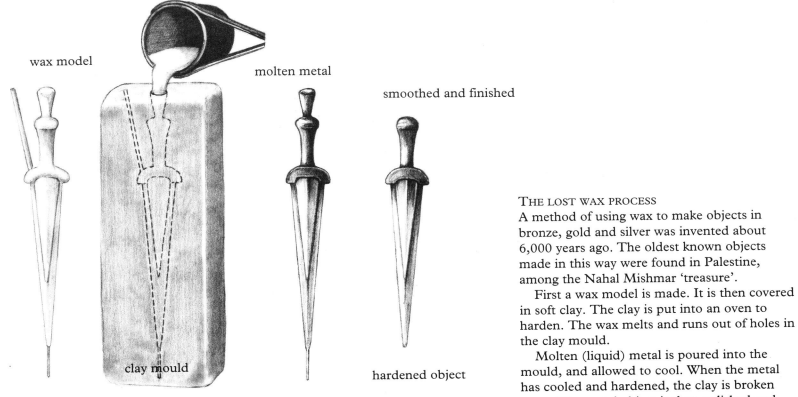

wax model

molten metal

smoothed and finished

clay mould

hardened object

THE LOST WAX PROCESS

A method of using wax to make objects in bronze, gold and silver was invented about 6,000 years ago. The oldest known objects made in this way were found in Palestine, among the Nahal Mishmar 'treasure'.

First a wax model is made. It is then covered in soft clay. The clay is put into an oven to harden. The wax melts and runs out of holes in the clay mould.

Molten (liquid) metal is poured into the mould, and allowed to cool. When the metal has cooled and hardened, the clay is broken away. The metal object is then polished and finished.

GLOSSARY

aboriginal original inhabitant of a region.

anthropomorphic similar to the human form.

archaeologist person who studies the past through remains of buildings, bones, fragments of pottery and so on.

aurochs wild cattle, larger than domestic breeds today but now extinct.

Azilian culture of prehistoric Europe (especially France and Spain), characterized by small stone tools and red and black paintings.

basalt rock formed by solidified volcanic lava.

bolas hunting weapon made from one or more thongs with stones tied to the ends, whirled around and then thrown at the prey.

bronze metal alloy of copper and tin.

cardial form of pottery decoration, made by pressing a shell into the wet clay. Named after a cockle, *Cardium.*

caste closed social group.

cereals food plants such as wheat, barley and rice, which yield grains that can be milled into flour.

Chalcolithic copper-using age.

clan social group formed by families with common ancestry.

community group of people living together and sharing a way of life.

cultivation planting and harvesting crops.

culture way of life, technology and thought of people in one area or at one time.

deity god or goddess.

dolmen burial monument made of two or more stones raised vertically, with another stone slab laid horizontally – like a tabletop.

domestic animals animals tamed for the farm (cattle, sheep, pigs, goats, chickens) or for work (dogs, camels, horses, asses, oxen).

drainage in prehistoric farming, getting rid of surface water by running it into ditches to dry the land for crop-planting.

dwelling building used as a home.

flexible easily bent or shaped by hammering.

flint stone used for making tools and weapons, by chipping or flaking away the edges.

hierarchy order of rank or importance of people within a group or tribe.

hunter-gatherers people who find their food by hunting or by picking wild fruits, leaves and berries.

Ice Age period when the climate cools and ice sheets extend from the polar regions.

impressed ware pottery decorated by pressing marks into the wet clay.

irrigation watering crops by digging ditches to divert water from a river around the fields or by other methods.

kiln oven for heating clay pottery.

malachite copper-containing mineral, bright green in colour.

megalith stone monument made from large slabs of stone.

Mesolithic name given to period between the Upper Palaeolithic and Neolithic ages.

migration movement of people or animals in large numbers.

millet edible plant with cobs formed from seeds.

monolith huge block of stone.

Four examples of prehistoric art, showing humans as hunters.

Far left: Two human figures, wearing animal masks or headdresses and carrying spears. Hunting period art from the Middle East.

Left: Goat depicted on pottery from Susa, about 4000-3000 BC.

Right: A picture from Arabia. The larger figure is carrying a bow.

Far right: Horned hunters with spears or darts and spear-throwers, from Mexico.

mound burial burial of the dead in a grave beneath a large mound of earth.

Neolithic the period of prehistory when people made polished or ground stone tools – roughly from 10,000 years ago.

nomads people who wander from place to place, either farming or herding flocks of animals.

obsidian volcanic black glassy rock, frequently traded in prehistoric times. It was used to make sharp cutting tools and knives.

Palaeolithic the period of prehistory when people made simple chipped-stone tools.

pasture grazing land suitable for grass-eating animals such as sheep and cattle.

patriarchy family or group organization based on father/male domination.

permanent staying in one place.

pottery objects such as pots, bowls and jugs made from wet clay hardened by heating in an oven or kiln.

rainforest forest of the warm equatorial regions, with all-year-round heat and high rainfall.

rape plant grown for its oil.

reaping cutting cereal plants in the field at harvest time.

rite religious or magical ceremony.

rock art paintings or engravings made on rocks or the walls of caves.

settlement place where people build permanent homes.

sickle curved cutting tool for harvesting cereals.

site location for archaeological investigation.

smelting separating metal from its ore by heating.

sorghum food plant belonging to the grass family.

statuette small statue, made from wood, clay, metal or stone.

status social and economic position, or rank within a community.

steppes grassy plains of east-central Europe and central Asia.

stylized drawing or sculpting figures in a particular way, not necessarily lifelike but always with the same essential elements shown.

temple building with a special religious or ceremonial purpose.

thatch bundles of reeds or straw, used for roofing a house.

tomb a burial place.

utensils household items such as bowls, knives, jars.

vetch herbaceous plant of the legume family, nowadays used as animal feed.

wadi dried-up river bed in the Sahara and other desert regions of Africa and Arabia. May fill with water when it rains.

INDEX